A Letter To My Bully:
Sticks, Stones, and Words Do Hurt

Sharisa T. Robertson

Arianna

Thank you for your support!
Good luck in school this
year and remember to be
a buddy not a bully!

A Letter To My Bully: Sticks, Stones, and Words Do Hurt

Unless otherwise noted, Scriptures are taken from *King James Version*.

ISBN: 978-0-9854961-2-8
Library of Congress Control Number: 2014919644

Published by Lilies of the Field Media, LLC Detroit, MI

Cover Design: Alegna Media Design, www.alegnamediasuite.com
Editing: Sara Dean, www.odesk.com
Book Layout: Sharisa T. Robertson

Printed in the USA

Lilies of the Field Media, LLC and its co-authors and contributors hope that you will find encouragement, inspiration, and information within the pages of this book. Happy reading and welcome to our world!

Presented To:

_____

From:

_____

Date:

_____

Dedication

Bullying is an illusion of power.
Being bullied is an illusion of being powerless.
Bearing witness to bullying and not speaking or not doing enough is an illusion that it is outside of your power to do something.
Behind it all, these illusions keep everyone from operating at their full potential, inner strength, and true power.

This book is dedicated to helping those young girls discover their true inner power and to ALL of the adults around them, the community that they reside in, and the schools that they attend, whose duty is to ignite that power and to teach, while also demonstrating to them how to be powerful, responsibly and positively.

Girls, you are powerful, you have a voice, you matter and someone around you is listening, cares, and is there to help!!!

Table of Contents

Foreword

After reading through the letters from young women in '*A Letter To My Bully: Sticks, Stones, and Words Do Hurt*', I am overcome with emotions that are difficult to describe. As these letters take on the bullies who have tormented these girls, I hear vivid cries from hearts filled with pain. But it is the overwhelming sense of triumph that has brought me to tears.

When victims find the courage to assert their humanity and address their tormentors, their fearlessness is a lesson to us all. The bravery of these girls to find the words and to share their experiences is an invitation for all of us to stand together.

In the midst of the anguish and heartbreak documented here are authentic testaments of empowerment, forgiveness, and spirit. Bullied children experience feelings of shame, desperation, isolation, and betrayal. But as they discover their voices and come to terms with their identities, they are taking a stand and growing in confidence and truth.

Girls have been bullied for all kinds of reasons - their hair, weight, or other issues about how they look, their culture or beliefs, their family, their grades, being different. Bullying hurts. It causes loneliness, depression, low-self esteem, division, difficulty with school, and contributes to fractured friendships, relationships, and families. Severe bullying can even result in suicide.

But by taking pen in hand, these young women decided to confront their feelings and their bullies and say, "No more! I'm not going to believe you anymore!" It's a heroic step that has far-reaching consequences. These voices inspire other girls to remember how they were created - as a gift.

I've been teaching girls, "You Are The Gift" for over ten years now. We were each endowed with unique beauty, inherent dignity and rights, because we were created in God's image. All we need to do is recognize that gift, and when we do, change happens inside and all around.

There are many phenomenal transformations I see when girls discover their gift status. Especially noticeable here are unity and seeing humanity in others. As these young ladies discover their worth and find their courage, they also begin to see that the divisiveness so common among pre-teen and teenage girls is deceit.

They begin to see other girls and other groups as allies and all the differences of others as unique gifts just like them. They see that no one needs to be the same to identify with one another. This togetherness is a huge leap in maturity and wisdom and helps bring healing bonds to young women and lets them participate in deep friendships.

At the same time, as they are walking away from their bullies, I see these girls affirming their humanity too. Many of these girls talk about the wounds that drive their tormenters. They know that their bullies are lonely, scared, hurt - human. While every girl is at a different stage of her journey, and each victim is wholly entitled to her anger and bitterness, the direction of healing always points to forgiveness and a deep hope for peace.

I am amazed at the tenacity, resilience and insight revealed in these letters. But I shouldn't be. God called me to work with young people many years ago, and every day I witness a determination to understand and overcome what is often grim reality. I see it every day, but it never loses its impact: the hope, faith, and love revealed through children. It is nothing less than the face of God's amazing grace.

Dr. Derschaun Monique Sharpley
President and C.E.O.
Helping Individuals Succeed (H.I.S.) Agency

Preface

As a parent, seeing your child, in my case children, being bullied is a difficult thing. You go through so many ranges of emotions. One minute you're angry and wish that you could ring the neck of the child that is hurting them, but then you wonder how can a child be so angry, what is going on in their life? The next moment you're sad because you see how it is really affecting your children, and you are not able to protect them while they are in school.

You're antsy throughout the day because you don't know if at that very moment while you're thinking about them, if someone is picking on them. As you wait for them to get out of school and to hope that the bullying has just disappeared, you ask the infamous question, *"How was your day?"* You hold your breath hoping that today was a good day. Sometimes it is, but most times it isn't.

I can't say that I know what they are going through, since being bullied is a new experience to me. I wasn't a popular child in school. I had friends but unless I knew you, I was usually very quiet. I had a few altercations with what we called, 'the dozens' back in the day, where we capped (that is what we called it when you talked about someone) on each other.

I was bullied for about a week by a high school girl when I was in elementary school. She would come to the neighborhood park and for whatever reason would punch me in the arm repeatedly, push me a few times, and say mean things to me. I admittedly didn't stick up for myself as I should have (I was scared because she was way older than me, and I had never been in a fight). I didn't tell my parents because I didn't want them to ban me from the park, so I stuck it out. She disappeared, so I was spared.

I always wished I had stood up for myself even if that meant being beat up, because essentially I was being beaten up by not saying anything. I always wondered if she hadn't disappeared if the bullying would have continued and what would I have done if it had.

Shortly after that, I decided that I wouldn't start any fights but if someone came to me, I would fight them. Wouldn't you know, I ended up fighting two brothers in the same week, standing up for myself. I was scared, but I did it, and I won too. That has been my motto in life. I had a few altercations but luckily I didn't have to fight (physically) too much in my younger days (I am not telling anyone to fight, I am just telling my experience and story).

What is a parent to do? These days just saying 'fight back' isn't always enough, because they can be suspended and what if your child doesn't want to fight? You tell them to ignore it, which only amplifies the bully to bully even more. You tell them to tell the teacher, you even come up to the school demanding something be done and be done immediately. Sometimes that works, sometimes it makes it worse but it does at least put everyone on alert about what is going on. Do you homeschool them? Do you get the authorities involved? Do you have them take karate classes? Or do you have them suck it up and "deal" with it?

I have even been guilty of getting upset with my children because I wanted them just to put an end to it. I couldn't understand in the beginning why it just kept happening and why they were being targeted all of the time. Their father and I confused them even more because they were trying to learn by taking our advice (which sometimes didn't fit into school rules that they tried hard to follow) on how to handle themselves and when to use what advice at what time. It was hard for them to figure out when they should just walk away, when they should stick up for themselves, and when they should tell. It seemed like when they did anything it made it worse and even may have gotten them in trouble and when they came home to tell us what happened, we would tell them sometimes they either didn't do enough or did too much.

Even though they continued getting good grades and achievement, seeing a decline in excitement about going to school and seeing some other behavior in your child(ren) that isn't normal, we try and be there for them and comfort them. We let them know that we will be there, and as their parent we will fight for them and on their behalf, and teach them the appropriate way to "fight" as well. We remind them how special they are, to stand up for themselves, and to always keep their head high. Is that enough? I don't know.

But what I noticed is that children need to know, especially when being bullied, that they are bigger than what is happening right now. They are more than a victim of bullying, that they are loved, that they matter, that they were not put here to be treated badly, and most importantly, that they have a voice.

A voice, in a world where bullying seems to be running rampant leaving many of the youth, our youth, voiceless. Even more so than ever before, school shootings, dropout rates increasing, and even children committing suicide because they are sick and tired of being bullied, our children have to know that they have a voice, that their voice matters, and that their voice is being heard. Just because someone, or maybe even a few people, may not appreciate what they have to say, it doesn't make it any less important.

So how can I give my children a voice and a jolt of confidence? How can I teach them that everybody will not like them nor will they like everybody and that is ok? How can I teach them it is about how they carry themselves, how they treat others, and how they allow (and teach) others to treat them? How can I allow them to have a productive release instead of bottling up their feelings? How can I show them how to take a stand for themselves against their bullies by saying what they have wanted to say, no interruptions, no judgments? How can they become advocates for others on a huge cause, because this isn't just about them but others? How can they let others into their world? How can I get other girls involved who can relate to being bullied for just being who they are?

That is how 'A Letter To My Bully: Sticks, Stones, and Words Do Hurt' came to be, a platform for them to directly confront their issues. Also to say what they need to say and what better way to do that than to be an author and take part in a book collaboration?

I am a strong believer in turning your pain into your purpose. I had to do it, and I wanted to teach my girls and other girls to do the same, and having the opportunity to learn how at a young age is even better. I wish I had that chance as a young girl when I was going through my hard times and needed to know my voice mattered.

This book answers all those questions and more. This book is a uniting of voices, perspectives, experiences, and a jolt of confidence as well. This book is a platform to a changing of lives for all of those involved and prayerfully for those who read it.

I struggled with bringing this book to life, but kept pushing through to completion because I want every person reading this to never let whatever hard times you may be going through make you stop believing.

Let it make you stronger. Let it make you take a stand. Let it make you find your voice. Let it make you help others. Let it make you be you, and only you, and to see yourself in a way that you may not have before - stronger.

I invite you to read '*A Letter To My Bully: Sticks, Stones, and Words Do Hurt*'.

Sharisa T. Robertson

Introduction

Bullying is nothing new. It has always been around for generations. But I think many would agree that the dynamics have changed dramatically. Bullying and school violence has increased and has become more of a threat due to technology and the way people, from adults to children, can handle their emotions and thoughts.

Knowing that my girls were being bullied and witnessing it get worse year by year, has been hard. Even if they went to a new school, or if we moved to a new neighborhood, it was apparent that more had to be done. Not just in regards to speaking out against bullying, but also how to deal with the emotional and mental aspect of being bullying. So for the sake of my children and other's I used a tool that had worked for me when I needed healing and has worked for many others – writing.

Writing has been a huge tool for me in dealing with my problems, sorting them out and sometimes it was the only way I could even have a voice in such a noisy place in our world. I always wrote in a journal as a child, and I stopped writing when I got older, but I always journal a bit and jot down my thoughts. It was my escape and my savior. A year before being blessed with the vision of doing this bullying book project, I did a book collaboration for women who have issues with their mother called, ‘*A Letter To My Mother: A Daughter's Perspective*’.

The women were able to achieve some healing, release, forgiveness, and have a voice. We had already started journaling with the girls at home, but they needed more. Then the idea graced upon me, why not do the same type of book project I did for the other women and myself who have a strained relationship with our mothers, and do one for my daughters, but make it an open project for others to join along. It made so much sense!

The title is so fitting because, yes, it is A Letter To My Bully, but we also know that bullying can be painful and hurtful physically, emotionally, and mentally. Sticks represent the emotional and mental hurt; Stones represents the physical abuse, and Words, of course, represents the verbal abuse.

So when we say 'Sticks, Stones, and Words Do Hurt' we are talking about every aspect of pain both seen and unseen. The wounds are painful and leave scars, visible and invisible. One isn't worse than the other; all are brutal and impact the child being bullied on so many levels, as you will see personally from reading this book.

When this book was just a project starting out, and I was looking for youth to join my two daughters in telling their stories, I didn't know what to expect, but I got exactly what I was looking for. *'A Letter To My Bully: Sticks, Stones, and Words Do Hurt'* takes you into the thoughts and experiences of seven courageous young girls from ages 9-14 years old.

But it doesn't stop there. There is also an expert bonus section within the book featuring strong adult female authors and contributors who have either experienced being bullied in their youth as well, had children who experienced bullying, or work with the youth who have had this type of behavior and issue. So whether from a professional or personal perspective, or a mixture of both, the adult contributors and authors add another element to this book by providing insight and information on this topic.

The expert section is so vital to this book. It includes stories of being bullied and overcoming it, lessons they learned from their experience, and how they turned their pain into their purpose. It also includes an interview from a psychologist answering questions that you may have been seeking answers to and giving a deeper insight from a psychological viewpoint of bullying not just from the victim, but also from the bully.

There is also a deep introspection of the way we are raising our kids and the necessary steps, (listed as tips for easy reference) we should take to produce emotionally stable, empathic, children with ideal characteristics and integrity. We have valuable nuggets in regards to bullying prevention/elimination, and the roles of everyone involved and/or affected by bullying within schools, families, and the community.

Just about every perspective goes back to the responsibility of the parent and adults, but mostly parents. This was not planned. I was blown away conducting the interviews and reading the contributions myself. It pinpoints one of the main common denominators, not to place blame but to speak truth, providing information and responsibility. We (parents and adults) are the answer to our children's problems, whether we know it or not.

Included also, are words of encouragement from successful women running a business and having a successful career working with young girls/children on a daily basis who have contributed to the foreword and afterword of this book.

'A Letter To My Bully: Sticks, Stones, and Words Do Hurt' is broken down into the following sections:

- Letters written from our youth authors to their bullies
- **I Affirm** section at the end where each girl states their affirmation(s), affirming who they are and standing tall in their identity and individualism. *To affirm is to state, to speak, to*

declare, to set intentions, to create, to take ownership, to believe, to work towards, and to become without doubt. Please feel free to use the affirmations and recite them every day until you believe them or come up with your own.

- Expert contribution based upon the professional and/or personal experience of five phenomenal women.

- Facts and Statistics to keep you informed and educated about bullying, including girl on girl bullying from several websites that we researched as well. Links are included for you to refer to as well for your research.

- Pledge against bullying for youth and adults to take, recite, remember and truly apply.

- Technology contracts for both parents and children that can be used and revised as needed to set a firm understanding of expectation in regards to all technology.

- Bonus section at the end where you or anyone you know that has been, or is being, bullied can write a letter to their bully and be an unofficial author to the book project as well and hopefully find a much needed release.

- And how exciting! We also have a theme song for this book project and our movement against bullying. TAJ, a 16-year-old artist from Atlanta, released her first single under Epic records; *"U CAN'T BULLY ME"* The song is a great compliment to ATLMB because music has a huge influence on us all, especially our youth. The fact that they now have a theme song about not being bullied is huge!! I am honored to have partnered with her! Check out the back of the book for details on how to download your copy of the hit.

This is what makes the book so special and different. These girls can write directly to their bully/bullies even if they are not exactly able to talk *directly* to their bully/bullies. So they are still able to say what it is they need to say and get it all out.

One of the young authors in the book has not been bullied but just wanted to speak out against bullying. She felt the need for us all to take part in ending bullying, and you don't have to be bullied to stand up and get involved. In reading these young girls' personal letters, maybe you can relate to their experience and find inspiration in their strength and fight against bullying.

Also, this book is special and different because it is not only a tool for those being bullied, but for bullies to maybe see what it is that they are doing to others. It also can be a great guide and conversation starter for teachers, principals, parents, communities, and for those who work with young girls. It can also be great for boys! It will serve as a great reference, as a tool for awareness as a conversation starter; give answers, solutions, and information.

After you read the firsthand testimonies and experiences in the letters and expert section make sure to read more about who the girls and ladies are in their bios. It has been a pleasure for me, learning about them and getting to know them.

I am honored and commend each young girl, parent, and expert who took part in making this vision an actual book in your hands. I am blessed that they not only trusted me, but included me in their journey and lives on such a big subject like this.

It took a bit of work to get this book together but it was worth it, and what makes it even more worth it is the fact that YOU are reading it right now because I know it will be a blessing to you in some way.

Enjoy! Become aware! Be informed! Be inspired! Start dialogue! Take some sort of action towards change!

Sharisa T. Robertson

Being Brave Even When I am Scared

Italia Samere Ventour

Dear Bully,

Remember when you called me white? It makes me feel sad. You always call me names. It makes me feel mad. It also makes me cry. It hurts me very badly. Remember when I was sitting in the lunchroom? And you came up to me and said I'm whiter than the floor? I went home and looked in the mirror and said to myself, *am I the right color?*

Why? Why do you have to pick me to pick on? Why? That's all I want to know. It made me feel bad about myself. I wanted to be darker. I use to ask my parents why was I so light, and everyone was brown or darker. I thought I was white. People would ask me if I had a different dad because I was lighter than everyone in our house. That always hurt my feelings, and I felt like I was different.

Do you remember when school first started in 2nd grade, the first day of school? I was talking to my mom; you came up to us and asked my mom, was I black? Later that day you and another girl said you were not my friends because I'm not a real black person. I went home to tell my Mom, and I cried for a real long time.

One time you stole my lunch, cussed at me, and hit me. I told my mom. She had to come up to the school. Another day, I was going up the pole during gym, and before I got to the top, you pulled me down by the neck and I fell flat on my back on the hard floor. So I told the teacher, and she didn't do anything about it.

I went back to play, and you tripped me and I fell. My money fell out of my pocket, and you took it and you took my chips. You would break my pencils in school, talk about me, and laugh at me. It was something every day and my mom had to come up to the school for stuff to be taken care of.

Even if you'd bully me I still try to be your friend. But you don't what to be friends. I just want to ask, why do you bully me? What did I ever do to you? Just tell me so I can fix it. Just tell me. I didn't even do anything to you.

That's how I feel when you bully me. When you bully me, I say to myself, *why did you pick me to bully?* I ask a lot of questions trying to figure out what is going on, but I can never figure out the answer.

I transferred to a new school, and I thought things would be better. But I was bullied again. People kept bullying me and calling me white even at the new school. I didn't do anything to any of you. Every time you call me white, I get mad and turn red like fire. All the students look at me like I'm crazy.

Then my sister started to bully me because she was getting bullied at her school. She didn't stick up for herself either, so she came home and took it out on me, punching and pinching me, yelling at me, pushing me, and pulling my hair. I started to write and draw pictures of me being beat up in my school journal, about what my sister was doing to me when my parents weren't looking, but eventually they found out, and she stopped.

I was even getting bullied on the bus too. It was real bad too. I ended up not wanting to go to school sometimes, and I love school, but I was sick of it and of all of you. At first I didn't stick up for myself because I was scared. I had never been in a real fight before, and I didn't want to get in trouble at school or home.

After so much bullying from people talking about me or putting their hands on me, the older I got, I got tired of being bullied. I started going to school and taking my anger out on people; even people who didn't do anything to me, just like my sister did to me.

I ended up getting into fights. One time I got suspended two times in one week. My parents were upset. I just had so much anger in me from so much stuff.

I decided to change my ways because I didn't want to always be in trouble and start things with people. I didn't want to do the bad things to others that were being done to me. I didn't want my mom and dad to be angry either. It didn't happen quickly, I still got in trouble some more and was still mean to my classmates but I did change eventually, because it didn't make me feel better.

Is that why you bully me, because you're mad about something too? Just tell me what I ever did to you? Just tell me why? I keep asking why because I really want to know. I am a nice person and would be a good friend, but you wouldn't know that because you're mean to me, or just won't leave me alone. I can't help the color of my skin, and I like being smart too.

I just learned we don't have to be friends or enemies. We don't have to talk to each other. I just learned that I don't have to listen to what people say about me. I love my skin. I don't care about what others say. I like my skin like this because I'm pretty and beautiful.

Black people come in all beautiful colors from light to dark. Just because I am light doesn't mean that I am a fake black person, or it doesn't mean that I have to have a different dad than my brother and sister because, we have the same dad.

God made me, and He loves me like I love Him. God will bless me so that I don't get bullied any more. Bullying is not our theme. So people should stop bullying each other. Sharing, caring and helping is the new theme. Bullying is out the door.

Loving the color that I am,

Italia

I affirm:

I am courageous, even when I am scared. *I love* the color of my skin.

About the Author

Already at 9, honor roll student, Italia Ventour has dreams of being a sculptor and creating whatever her vivid imagination leads her to. She is also considering being a police officer so she can help people.

She loves to read, especially comic books and mysteries. When she isn't reading, Italia likes to take cardboard boxes and make bookmarks and houses. She loves to draw and likes to mold clay (sculpting). She also loves watching TV, playing with her siblings of which she is the middle child out of 4, playing outside, and she has really begun to like playing basketball also.

Italia Ventour was born and raised in Detroit/Metro Detroit area. She knows being an author at such a young age is a huge accomplishment and appreciates her parents for helping her become one, especially since being bullied bothered her.

An All Natural Story

Justine Adams

Dear Tormentor,

Allow me to re-introduce myself. Hello, my name is Justine. I'm 14 years old, and I have all natural hair. Now I know 'tormentor' sounds pretty harsh but that is what you are, right? Sure feels like it to me, because you're tormenting me so much because of my natural hair. I didn't know how else to address you because really, "bully," seemed to do you no justice. That is how I view you, that is how you treat me, and that is how I felt - tormented by a tormentor.

You can describe my hair as very thick and extremely curly. I love my hair, but unfortunately people like you antagonize me for the way it looks. Most of the girls I know that are my age wear weaves, a perm, or their hair flat ironed. I'm pretty sure I'm the only girl in my school that wears my hair all natural.

Now because my hair is all natural, I wear it in a variety of styles. Sometimes I wear my hair in braids. Other times, I choose to wear it in twists, two braids, or just simply a twist out, with my curls bouncing around. I think my favorite style might be a twist out. I like the way my curls look. Occasionally, I may accessorize them with a headband or a flower.

However, even though I love my natural hair, I still get bullied for it. Regardless of the fact that I'm very confident in myself, I do get self-conscious when people talk about me. I've had you say my hair looks like worms, ramen noodles, cheese curls, and my hair is ugly overall. You've said my hair is short, but you never saw the real length of my hair. However, I've also had admirers compliment me on how beautiful my hair is and how unique I am for wearing my hair all natural.

I find it very amusing, the fact that oppressors, such as yourself, love talking about everyone else, when you don't even have your own selves together. I've had females come up to me talking about my hair, when they had a bad perm, horrible edges, and a nonexistent hairline. I've also had males with crummy haircuts talking about my hair. I've also had you suggest things on what to do with MY own hair, while your hair looks a hot mess!

I feel as though it isn't fair to judge others, when you aren't better than any one person in this world. Does it make you feel better to put others down? If your answer to my question is "yes," then you need some serious re-evaluating. Judging someone else, to only 1-up yourself isn't good for your self- esteem and self-confidence. How exactly would you feel if multiple people nagged you and attacked you just because you chose to wear a certain hairstyle that YOU were comfortable with?

Exactly.

Let me talk about you and put you down like you did me. Do you know how much I would've loved sharing my comments about what I thought about you? But no, I know what it feels like to be put down, and I decided that I would never want another person to experience that.

I further find it amusing, the fact that when I straightened my hair, you and the rest of your fellow oppressors were suddenly my friends and had all of these compliments to grant me. *"Oh, em gee Justine! Look at your hair!," "Wow, I didn't know your hair was that long." "You look so pretty,"* etc.

Now please excuse my arrogance, but I knew all of this already; yes my hair, is long, full, voluminous, bouncy, and I am quite attractive, if I do say so myself. Thanks for the compliments, but I know they're just artificial. Why did you have all those compliments then, but when my hair was all curly and natural, you only had criticism and disapproval to relinquish?

You made jokes about me, and yes, it's true I laughed along. But later on I realized it wasn't because I thought it was funny, but for the mere reason that I needed to laugh off my embarrassment. Being picked on can be humiliating. You never know what a person goes through during their personal lives. You don't know what attachment, that single person you're humiliating, could have to a single word.

All those words, which you harshly spit out onto that one different person, could end up having an unrelenting repetition in their head all day, causing them to cry themselves to sleep every night. You never know what goes on behind closed doors. That one girl you bullied because she didn't have the new Jordan's or a pair of Trues, may just decide to end her life that same night. Do you want to be the cause of such a terrible situation like that?

What you may not know is that I have second guessed myself because of things you said about me. I've sat in the mirror and thought things like, *"Would I look prettier with a perm?"* and *"What if I did get a weave?"* I've even beaten myself up because of things you said in that ceaseless bonfire of harsh jokes: *"Why won't my hair stay in one position?* "And *"Why couldn't I be normal and get a weave like other kids?"* But then I realized, I'm better than that.

The fact of the matter is I'm different from everyone else. There's only one Justine E. Adams in the world, and there would never be anyone that can replace me. If I want to wear my hair a certain type of way, that's my decision. No one can tell me or persuade me otherwise. My decisions are what make me unique from everyone else.

Your tormenting ways only made me stronger. I'm even more confident in myself. When someone comments on my hair, I just tell them that it's MY hair, and I'm still going to look beautiful even if I shave all of it off. I can wear my hair in braids, twists, straight, curly, etc. but that's what gives it its versatility. I love my natural hair no matter what. But what really matters is what's inside, not what your image is. Just thought you should know that.

My hair isn't the only thing you've picked on. You picked on my forehead just because it pokes out; called me a whore because boys find me attractive, even tried to call me dumb. However, I find it amusing that I'm comfortable with all of my flaws. Calling me names because the boy you were crushing on, asked me out, is just pure jealousy. It's also extremely amusing that you claim I'm "dumb", but I was accepted to multiple gifted schools, the National Junior Honor Society, earned numerous academic certificates and achieved Distinguished Honor Roll more times than you can count.

I can recall the day when you decided to throw me in the trash. Yeah, it might have been funny at that exact moment, but you never know how that incident still affects me to this day. Every time I think about it, I break down in tears. I couldn't look my parents in the eye, or anyone for that matter. So many people witnessed that, and the whole situation just kept replaying in my mind. I've had nightmares; and I rarely even get nightmares!

I've lost so many friends because they were untrustworthy. I didn't know who my real friends were for awhile afterwards. Too many, "he said, she said," made me feel torn and unwilling to believe anyone. I remember I cried for days afterwards; it was just so humiliating. I didn't want to go to school for a while, but I decided to go because I'm stronger than that. For awhile, I asked myself, *Why me? Why me out of all people?"*

After that and still to this day, I can't trust people. I don't know who to trust anymore because I've had some of my "friends" switch up on me before. You also took a big piece out of my confidence for awhile too. But in the long run, you only made me stronger.

So as I close out this letter, I just want to remind you, I am Justine E. Adams in the flesh. I will always be Justine E. Adams. There will always be one Justine E. Adams because I was made an original, not a copy. There's nothing or no one that will ever in a lifetime take that away from me; most especially not you. I will be confident in myself because your words are nothing but a mere blur in this fast paced world that I'm in.

One day, one very special day, I'm going to make it big. Someone, somewhere will discover me, and I'll be successful. Forget the money, cars, clothes, and fame because I will always be me. I just hope that one day, you will be happy for me.

When you see me making it big, I hope you realize that it's me out there. That one girl that you used to relentlessly antagonize is out there being her. Look how beautiful she looks. Don't you regret that day you called me those repugnant words? Goodbye Tormentor, and always remember that your words are now a day of the past. I'm moving on in my life, WITHOUT YOU.

Rocking my natural crown,
JustBeingJustine

I Affirm:

I am successful; *I turn* my adversities into opportunities.

I am winning. *I stand* up to what I believe.

My Kinky Hair is Beautiful.

I am Beautiful, Kinky hair, *and* all.

About the Author

Born in Brooklyn, New York, Justine Adams has always loved to read. She fell in love with stories before she'd even started Kindergarten. From a younger age than most, she found herself engrossed in books and was rarely seen without one, a fascination that would follow her through her life to where she is today- a rising sophomore at Moyer Academy. That love of reading led to her passion for writing, one that was expressed as early as the third grade, when she would spend her evenings after school writing and illustrating her own stories. As she moved up through the grades, her love pushed her to join up with a journalist club, which led to an opportunity of being featured in the New York local paper, AM New York, speaking on recycling.

Reading isn't her only passion. An accomplished dancer, she's garnered awards for ballet, tap, and jazz dancing, as well as several for her gymnastics and track records. She proved her range when she picked up prizes for Most Academic and Most Artistic, displaying her aptitude for both the inventive and the practical side of her school career. Justine was also one of the eighth-grade finalists in a statewide Art Postcard competition, placing first place in her category. On the honor roll from pre-K through Kindergarten (where she was valedictorian) to ninth grade, Justine- who'll be turning fifteen in December- wasn't simply satisfied with her academic achievements and began to look outside school for ways to express her skills and passions.

She was inducted into the National Junior Honor Roll in 6th grade; Justine is also an Archonette in the Epsilon Rho Zeta chapter of Zeta Phi Beta. Through this, she's reached out to the community in a variety of ways, feeding the homeless and completing STEM courses. She also began to investigate the world of arts and crafts, applying her entrepreneurial spirit and artistic talent to creating and selling duct tape creations. Forming the idea back in 2012, while trying to come up with the perfect Valentine's Day gift, she's crafted and sold everything from handbags to roses to wallets as Justine D'Artist.

As part of her 2014 summer break, she has enrolled in an Entrepreneurship program through Learning Curve M3 Accelerator where she is studying startups and entrepreneurship.

Justine combined her artistry with her own experiences, and, as a result of being bullied, designed a T-shirt defending natural hair. After the success of these, "Don't Judge a Girl By Her Hair" shirts scored, she turned her attention to taking further action against bullying. In recent months, Justine has decided to take a stand against bullying, applying her wit and her passion for writing a new book. In letters from Justine and other contributors, she addresses those children who bully, with plans to rally young people today to treat each other with more respect, care, and understanding. Her fundraising will go towards publishing this book, as well as organizing events in her community to raise awareness and strengthen the fight against bullying.

Being Bullied Has Made Me Stronger and Successful

Clara Huff

Dear Bully,

I remember when I first came to school. It was three months into the start of school. I was the quiet and shy, yet friendly, girl trying to make friends. All my life up until entering this school, I had been in New York. I left my foundation of BFFs, close friends and schoolmates of 11 years when I relocated to my mom's hometown. So connecting with other kids was very important to me. Several girls immediately befriended me. One of them quickly became my best friend, too.

During lunch and when we had recess, she and I would spend time drawing anime characters, working on our comic strip and laughing it up. She could trust me, and I could trust her. We were so much alike. We shared the same interests and wanted to do similar things in life. That's why we were so close. She was kind to me, and she made me laugh. That's what friends are for. But then you started causing problems. You started spreading rumors about me and my BFF. How could you accuse me of "liking" my best friend because we hung out a lot, and we were close? I didn't do anything to you to deserve this humiliation. I barely even said anything to you unless it was class related, and we had to work on a group project together. I wonder if you told lies because you secretly wished that you were as close to someone as I was to my BFF.

If you wanted to be my friend, all you had to do was be my friend and not be a rumor spreader. Our classmates started talking about us just because of the lies you told, and they began looking at us funny. It made my BFF cry, and it made me very angry. I was raised to treat people like I wanted to be treated. I would never want someone to say lies about me, and I definitely would not spread rumors about others. I believe that if you don't have anything nice to say about someone, you shouldn't say anything at all.

For what you did, I consider you a real coward. If you don't have the guts to say things to my face then don't say them at all. If somebody were to talk trash about you behind your back, you would be hurt too.

Thinking back on how I acted in class and the grades I received, as well as how much our teacher liked me; it makes me think that you were jealous. You see, I act like a young lady and I am polite. I don't shout out in class, and I am not disrespectful. I don't cause trouble, and I stay out of trouble. I am not always trying to know who is saying what about someone else. I am not trying to find out who likes who and who likes me. Actually, this was how you behaved. I survived 5th grade and received lots of class awards.

I thought that when I entered 6th and 7th grade things would be a lot better. But here you go again. I am not the typical teenager and because of that I think you tried to use this to bully me. I am a Christian. I love God, and I strive to serve him by following the Bible, attending church, and helping others. Because of this, I don't curse or hang in boys' faces trying to be fresh. I don't wear tight clothes, and I don't try to start fights. And, I don't listen to music that is negative, degrades women and talks about killing and robbing people.

I listen to positive and gospel rock music. In case you didn't know it, it's cool to be a Christian girl. As a visual and performing artist, I love going to plays and museums. My style is my own. I don't follow your ideal of style. I create my own to fit my personality. I don't appreciate it when you talk about what I am wearing. I wear what I like.

Do you see me talking about the inappropriate clothes that you wear? No. And, I don't judge you because of them.

You tried to make me feel like I was a loser or that I wasn't good enough to fit your standards. You tried to get other girls in on your bullying ways by encouraging them to whisper about me while I was sitting at my desk. But in case you didn't know it, I am in school to learn not to deal with nonsense. It is very difficult to concentrate when you hear people whispering your name and pointing at you as they are talking, then giggling. I tried to stick it out, but it was just too much. I would come home crying because all I wanted to do is learn and be friends with good people. I don't have to be friends with people who do not share my interests. Why would I want to be friends with you or the girls you hung with when all you did was be negative?

You say that I'm boney. So what? God designed me to be the height and weight that I am. If I am okay with being "slim", then what business is it of yours? Stop calling me names like this because they are not who I am. Don't try to make it seem like something is wrong with me.

This is a piece from a monologue I wrote called 'Ghost'. To cope with the hurt and pain due to your torture, I have been writing poems and songs about you. I have read about too many kids my age who have taken their own lives because they were bullied and didn't feel like they mattered. I even heard of kids cutting themselves and doing other bodily harm thinking it would erase the pain and make things better. I have become an advocate for those who have experienced bullying because like others, I too have suffered self-bodily harm and starving myself to push pass it. I hope to help other young people like me to begin to speak up about their bully experiences.

"There have been people who turned their backs on me
Telling people lies about me all because I was different
Had success and hope for myself
I cry hoping someone will take the people who wronged me away
To a place where they can feel my pain
Being left out on fun things like I'm a ghost
Forgotten that I exist and what I mean to people
I'm not a ghost
I'm a human being."

As a cheerleader, you bullied me through alienation. You purposely excluded me from conversations and girl powwows during breaks at practice and games. You saw me sitting by myself and instead of welcoming me, you gathered in your group and left me out. You would rush to chat with the other girls and even when standing beside me you would make your way around me to talk to the person next to me – but not me. You made me feel like I was a ghost. It didn't feel good being left out.

All I wanted to do was cheer our team on to victory and be a part of happiness. But, your blatant alienation left me alone and it felt bad. There is nothing wrong with me. I am a good person and I matter. No one should ever feel like this.

You really hurt my feelings by the actions you chose to take. What it also did was make me go deeper within myself, so that I could find the strength to stand tall even when I felt broke down with pain.

I don't hate you or people like you. I actually feel sorry for you. You have to be really unhappy with yourself to want to cause hurt, harm, and pain to someone else just because they are different or not a part of your crew. If you would concentrate on spreading love and getting to know people, and not gossip, this world would be a better place.

And, just to let you know, I don't want to be in your crowd. I don't need to live up to your standards. I am cool with me and the crowd that loves and accepts me for who I am — a loving, educated, athletic, gifted, and caring child of God. I know that I am somebody and have a lot to offer my school, the community, and this world.

Now that I don't have fear of you, I'm trying to make sure nobody else will feel or suffer the way you once made me feel. So I am standing tall and speaking up. I am spreading love not gossip. I am making a difference and giving hope to those young people who don't feel like they have a voice.

I pray that you will get yourself together. Take a look in the mirror and deal with those things that are hurting you. I have learned that hurt people hurt others. Life is too short for bullying. So, cut it out.

Spread Love, Not Gossip,

Clara Huff

I Affirm:

I am different, *and* *I'm* cool with that.

About the Author

At 14 years old, Clara Caasi Sharhran Huff is a jack of many talents and a master of them all. As the Founder & Artistic Director of My Budding Picasso Art (www.mybuddingpicassoart.com), she creates anime drawings, acrylic paintings, cartoon characters, comic strips and other art expressions with passion and precision. Clara has volunteered her artistic services to provide face painting for Powerhouse Media Group's 1st Annual Back-to-School Supply Giveaway (August 17, 2013) and for a cookout fundraiser to benefit a kidney transplant patient (August 24, 2013). She donated original acrylic paintings to the following causes: Youth Matter Inc.'s 5th Annual Black & White Gala Fundraiser (November 30, 2013) and KMK Production's Heartbeat Gala (February 7, 2014). Clara's artwork can be seen on Facebook under, "My Budding Picasso Art by Clara Huff."

Her love for visual arts has led her to a life in performing arts. In June 2013, Clara made her debut performance in the stage play, "Tailor Made." She played the role of Mabel, a teen fashionista and the favored daughter. Clara recently penned a monologue entitled, "Ghost", which speaks from the voice of a teen being bullied through alienation. She is dedicated to helping youth speak out against bullying. She is a featured youth author in Lilies of the Field Media, LLC's book project "A Letter to My Bully."

Clara is a proud AVID student at Indian River Middle School where she was a member of the cheerleading and track teams (2012-2014) and plays the violin in the orchestra and the flute in band. Last school semester, Clara qualified for the Citywide finals in the 1600M and 800M. She was selected for All-City Orchestra in 2013. She is the 2012 award recipient of Teens With a Purpose's "Move Maker Award." In June 2013, Clara won the title "Most Photogenic" at Phenomenal Women's Glam & Glitz Beauty & Scholarship Pageant in New York.

Clara conducted her first youth workshop, "Expressing Emotions Through Art with Clara Huff" this past July at a girls empowerment conference on the Eastern Shore (VA). She is a member of She'Matters G.I.R.L.S., LLC and a participant in The Betty Shabazz Delta Academy Program through the Chesapeake-Virginia Beach Alumnae Chapter of Delta Sigma Theta Sorority, Inc. as well as People Helping Our Youth Every Day. She was crowned Miss Youth Matter Teen 2013, where she serves as an ambassador for the nonprofit organization Youth Matter, Inc. She is a member of the Southeastern Virginia Arts Association. On October 6, 2014, Clara was awarded the Youth Crime Prevention Award at the 22nd Annual Crime Prevention Awards Ceremony in Norfolk, VA, by the City of Norfolk, the Citizens Police Academy Alumni Association of Norfolk and the Norfolk Police Department for her efforts to combat bullying.

Clara is proud of the skin that she's in and doesn't have the desire, nor feel the need, to be anyone but her. She is colorful, animated, joyous, daring and unconventional. Her motto in life is: "Different is Beautiful."

Too Much Trust

Chante N. Whisonant

Dear Bully,

Before I was bullied, I felt fine. I was happy; I wasn't insecure, I didn't feel fat, I didn't feel worthless, I didn't feel "white as snow". But when I started getting bullied that all changed. I started getting bullied in first grade, on my first day! I was sitting in class. Then I saw you. I wanted to be friends, but I was scared to say 'Hi.' I was always a shy girl. Later at lunch I was by myself until you came over. You said 'Hi, I'm LG', and I smiled and said 'I'm Chante.'

After that day we became best friends. No one could rip us apart…at least I thought. I was waiting for you by my locker. I saw you come to me. "Hey!" I yelled happily.

Then you looked different. "Look Chante, we can't be besties anymore."

The "cool kids" started snickering.

I was shocked, hurt, and sad. I asked you why not, your answer was I wasn't "Cool" like you anymore. Then you pushed me down hard and laughed then walked away. I ran to the bus stop, got on the bus, and held my tears in till I got home. Then I got off the bus, ran inside my home and cried. I just told my mom I had a bad day.

The next day I went to school; I sat by myself. I was minding my own business, not bothering anyone. Then you walked into class. You said "Hey! It's motor mouth!" then the whole class started to laugh. I just put my head down. But it got worse later. At break time in class, I was coloring a robot for my mommy. You came to me and ripped it apart! You stuck your tongue out at me, saying, "Aww poor baby."

A tear slipped down my cheek. I didn't understand; I won't understand. Why, why would you do this? What made you do this? I thought we were friends! I was wrong; nobody's friends with "motor mouth." It was time to go home. I was so happy to go home. I got on the bus singing.

Then you again came up to me and said, "The piggy can sing!? I didn't know that. Because most of the time, you're stuffing your mouth. You're probably so light because you drink so much milk." Even though it didn't make sense, it still hurt. Then you started making piggy sounds. I held my tears in.

My mom always said, "Don't let them see you cry." So I didn't. You know that saying, 'sticks and stones may break my bones, but words may never hurt me?' It's a lie. Words hurt **a lot.** More than you would think actually. It feels like a knife stabbing you in the heart.

I told my grandma about the bullying and **begged** her not to tell my mom and dad. My grandmother said, "Keep your head up". I tried but it was very hard. Soon after, things got worse and worse with you. You'd kick me, curse at me, pull my hair, and rip up my stuff. And it continued through first grade. I was still confused. How could you? All I wanted was your respect.

I couldn't wait for the summer! No bullies, no teasing, just fun. Summer was great! I was at a new school! I was so happy never to see you again. But then second grade came...and oh boy...

I met you KD. Again, you were nice to me at first, then things changed. Do you remember that day in class everybody was waiting for the teacher? I was just in my own little world. Then you started hitting and slapping me and the class was yelling, "Fight, fight, fight!" I was getting tired of this, and I started fighting back. But, of course, when the teacher came you blamed it on me. And everyone was too scared of you to say something.

I was in trouble…for defending myself! I was mad; I was confused. The school called my parents and said I started the fight. And you said I was bullying you! But my parents know I would never do **anything** like that. No matter what, I would never bully someone. No one deserves to feel stupid, ugly, fat, and useless. No one…

My parents were proud of me for fighting back! So was I. But that fight didn't stop you though, it just made you angrier! Why? Because you didn't get your way this time. That fight made things really bad. You'd pull my hair. You spit on me. You kicked me.

I hated you.

Again I trusted you. I asked you one day why…just why? You said I was **"Too nice. You're easy to walk all over. You look like a boy really. I never liked you fatty. It was all a game."** Then you started laughing. I ran away and cried. Every day you would beat me up for no reason.

I remember that day you grabbed a boy's hands, and made him… touch….me. "Stop!" I yelled. But he was weaker than you. And I was backed up into a corner, trapped. I somehow got away and ran to my house, and told my parents everything.

Things got so bad with you we had to call the police! But your mother wouldn't listen. You were so innocent in her eyes. More like the queen of lies. I hated my life. But guess what, you moved! I was so happy I couldn't tell you how I felt. And I thought everything was going to be fine again. Wrong.

I finally made a new (trustworthy) friend, RP; we hung out all the time. We were walking to the bus, and a boy came over. He said get off "his" bus stop. I said no. Then he pushed me down hard. I cried. My friend quickly came to help me. "Are you okay Chante'?!" I nodded.

You flashed a fake smile and then yelled, "Why did you do that R!!!?" You R, came to us and pushed her. You said, "Watch your back." Things went bad again.

There was a boy at school bullying me, and you were bullying me! It was horrible. I didn't get it. Why me? Why? I have always been a good girl! Love others, pray. I even prayed for you. Remember when you kicked me? Remember when you spat on me? Remember when you said I was lighter than snow? I had to deal with you and the other kids.

Getting on the bus, already wanting to go home, I got off and walked into my classroom. My sweet teacher welcomed me. She was so very nice to me. She always called me her fave student. We were practicing for a school play! I got the lead role!

CM, you, my other bully wasn't happy. I felt pain swim through my body. CM, you threw a chair at my back! I fell on the floor crying. "You only got it because she felt sorry for you." You yelled.

Then you started punching me. Over, and over, and over. Gasps filled the air. The teacher quickly grabbed you and got you off me. I could hardly move! My teacher helped me to the school nurse. The school nurse loved me too. Seeing the teacher and nurse always made me happy. The teacher told the nurse everything and left. The nurse laid me down and started telling me to pay my bullies no mind. Easy for her to say.

My mom and dad came and picked me up. I blocked out their complaining and just started thinking this is the worst day of my life. And guess what? We lived in the same building. That's why every day I would walk around the neighborhood to avoid you. My mom told me to stop doing that. But I couldn't. I would get in trouble for doing it every day. But I never stopped. I couldn't tell her. They would worry a lot.

I actually started to bully myself. "No one loves you. Motormouth, you're fat, ugly, and dumb." Every day I would say that. Then second grade ended, and I never saw you, CM again. But you, R, you still bullied me in 3rd grade! One day you and your brother jumped me! I ran inside my home and hid my crying face from my mom and dad. I locked the door. I was so tired I was done with life. I cried some more, then I wiped my tears and wrote a note:

Dear Mommy and Daddy,

I'm sorry, but I'm tired of getting bullied every day. And you try to help but the school won't listen. So I'm going to end it. I wrote this to say I love you and bye,

Love, Chante

I tried cutting myself but...but it just hurt too much. But it did leave a mark. I put my hands to my throat and squeezed really tight till I couldn't breathe anymore. Everything started going blurry, but I thought how I would hurt my mom and dad, and I stopped. I started coughing really hard. My grandmother started banging on the door. "Are you okay?" she asked, but I couldn't answer, I was still coughing hard. I chocked out a yes.

I got the note I wrote, ripped it up really small and threw it away. I started crying again. Why did you do this to me? Why would you drive me to this point?! I never did anything to you. I tried to be nice! I tried to make you understand! It never worked! I went outside crying. I yelled to the sky! "WHY GOD? WHAT HAVE I DONE? YOU DON'T LOVE ME NO MORE!"

But, of course, no one loves me, how could you? Soon as you saw me you'd probably puke. This is what I thought. I ran inside before anyone saw me. I went inside and put my mommy's makeup on to cover my scar. Then I put a band-aid on. And I put on a long-sleeved top. If asked what it was, I would say I fell.

Next day you and your brother tried jumping me again. This time my daddy was there. I snapped and started fighting back. You threw me against the car. Pain spread through my body. My dad came got you and your brother off me. My dad took me in the house and told my mother. My mom and dad were finally tired of it and took me to the principal's office and took me out of school.

I was so happy! No more bullies, no more being jumped, no more fake friends. I was relieved. I skipped out of school a happy girl. My mom and dad started homeschooling me. I really liked it. I didn't have to deal with ignorance anymore.

Then we moved to B'more. And my mom's friend had a daughter just a little younger than me, you SP. We played and hung out kind of often. I was starting to like you a lot. About three months into our friendship, you invited me to your birthday party. I couldn't wait to go! My mom left me at your house. I got into the door, and you greeted me. We were having a lot of fun until you invited your other friend over.

She started hitting me, throwing basketballs at the back of my head, and started calling me names. You didn't help me! You just stood there! I asked you to say something. You just walked away. I ran upstairs and sat on the couch. Your mother asked me if I was okay. I lied and said yes, then nodded. But I got bored and went back downstairs, and you started doing it again.

Hours passed. And my mom came and picked me up. I faked a happy goodbye and left. Soon as we got in the car, I busted out crying, and I told my mother everything. And I didn't talk to you anymore.

Why do all my 'friends' do this? I guess I'm too desperate for friends. My parents always told me: "Just because they are nice, doesn't mean they're your friends." And I wish I had listened to that. My mom and dad worked; I had no siblings around me, so I'd put up with anything for friends I guess.

A couple of years passed. I had a good amount of friends by then. I was happy, no teasing, no fat piggy names. Me, just being happy. The only problem I had was this group of girls who didn't like me at all.

You all would say mean things and use foul language. But it never really bothered me. Until one day, you girls and my friends got into a big fight. After that, you became REALLY mean. That's when the new girl came to the neighborhood.

You KW, you were cool and nice at first. We weren't really friends, but you were okay. But then you started hanging out with that group of girls. I didn't care because now I fought back a lot more. But one against four?! There's no way I could fight all of you alone.

Remember that day in June? I was playing with my BFF. You came to me and took my scooter and threw it on the ground. The reason? One of the girls in your 'group' lied on me.

You picked me up by my collar and threw me to the ground! And you started kicking me and punching me as my BFF was yelling stop. I was trying to fight back. You were a better fighter. Fighting is the last thing I would want to do, but if I have to I will.

I got up with blurry vision, and held my arm. You smirked evilly. And you made your lil' brother punch me two times in my stomach. You always bullied him, always made him cry. You're evil; you're two-faced, you don't deserve friends! I hit you hard and ran to your house, with my BFF behind me. My BFF and I told your mother **everything;** she couldn't believe it.

Then you came up to your door, with shock written all over your face. You tried to lie and said you were protecting your lil' bro. I called him and asked what happened. And guess what? He told on you! Your mouth was shut. Later, before we went to church, we went to your house. You got in more trouble. Haha!! I was trying to hold my laughter in. You gave me death glares, but I didn't care!

After that, you wanted to be friends, but I said no. You want to know why? You're two-faced. Fake. And I don't do that. You soon left me alone. But your group didn't. You guys tried to get me to talk about my best friend! Really?! After I said, I would never do that,   you got really mad. You cussed at me. You called **me** fake? I'm fake? Yeah, whatever.

You started hitting my friend in the back of the head, repeatedly. I yelled "Stop!" And I kicked you. My best friend was crying. I held her and said if you touched her again I would kill you. You called me foul language and were going to hit me. I snapped. I grabbed you and threw your body on the ground hard. The girls started screaming. I couldn't believe I did that! I was so happy.

My dad was down the street, just watching me defend myself and my best friend who couldn't fight. You moaned in pain and started crying loudly. The girls started running away, except my friend. You got up and acted like you were leaving and kicked me down. Then we started fighting. Of course, I won! And then you limped home.

My friend and I explained everything to my parents. After that day, you would literally stalk me. Write on my house. Challenge me. Walk around my house, like, 50 times a day to get me aggravated. You'd harass my parents too! You would bother my other friends, my neighbors. It was crazy!

One day I was in my house looking out the back screen door. You came around. I rolled my eyes and tried to ignore you. You stood in my yard, and you were staring into my house! And made funny faces and pretended to punch my face. I got mad and yelled at you to move from my house! My mom came to see what was going on. She went outside and started yelling at you to finally stop harassing us! You went home and came back with your mother.

You lied and said my mother called you a bad word. My mouth hung open. Then the other group of girls came and started a big fight with everyone. And the police came and told you guys to stay away from here. Your mother believed you. The other mothers were mad at their kids. Months passed and things never changed with you, but you moved! I was jumping for joy with my friend! I never, ever, ever, ever had to see you again!

Soon the rest of your 'group' moved too. I thought everything was **finally** fine, nope. One more hit. Last year. I was chatting in the back of my house with my friends one day. And a boy came over. I kind of knew him. I had a **BIG** crush on him. Hey S, I said happily. He started laughing and teasing me. Why S? I...I thought you liked me back. At least you said you liked me awhile back. My mom warned me about you. But I didn't listen.

You said horrible stuff to me, things that were sexual in nature, and inappropriate, and rude. Then you and your friends started laughing. I kept trying to change the subject because you knew I didn't like it, but you kept on and on. 'I could never date you, you know why? I don't date Elephant's!,' you said. My friends were trying to get you to stop except my BFF's brother. We were friends too, but he was joining in with you. My lil' heart was crushed. I just sat there at **my house** and listened to you talk about me.

I felt stupid! You made me insecure! I hate you! I liked you! You gained my trust and threw it away. You knew I liked you! Was it all a game? Huh? I wish you could answer me! My life is a game! I made you leave my house finally. I told my mom and dad and I broke down crying. You said sorry. But still, I couldn't forgive you. I always said I trust people too quickly. You know, I have learned from these experiences.

I love being homeschooled now; the transition was kind of hard at first. My mother is kind of strict when it comes to homeschooling, but I like it. When I go back to public school for high school, I won't be afraid anymore. Those years being homeschooled helped me work on myself a lot... I will no longer be that scared girl. Remember, trust God not man.

I defend myself now. After thinking it all over, I know what my problem was. I was too desperate for friends. I grew up in a Christian, all adult household, so I was always a little more mature and other kids didn't like that I guess. For a while I had some trust issues. But I can't hide forever.

I don't let people walk all over me. I speak my mind. Physical fighting is not always the answer. Never fight fire with fire. I'm not scared anymore. To quote Taylor Swift "Someday I'll be living in a big ol' city, and all you're ever going to be is mean."

I learned don't let them bring you down. It keeps hurting if you keep allowing it. Never be a victim. But never become the bully either. Some people are so scared of being bullied they become a bully. That's what happened to one of my friends. She was in that "group" of girls. She became so scared that she became a bully. I didn't know her anymore.

Some people bully because it gives them power. Power to see you cry. Power to see you scared. Power to see they have you wrapped around their fingers. Don't give them that power!

Some bully because they have a horrible life at home. So they want everybody else to feel their pain too. That's not the answer either! If you are scared to fight back, tell somebody! This is not okay! It will keep happening if you allow it to happen!

Never let anyone bring you down. Never try killing yourself or self-harm. You're just giving them what they what. Never let someone have that much power over you. You are worth so much! Think about your mom and your dad and your whole family! They love you! God loves you! If they don't know you are being bullied, tell them. They will try and help you. You never know till you try.

If you are scared, know that God is there to help you! You can't talk to Mom, can't talk to Dad, talk to Him! He understands. He always has been there for you. You just never asked for His help.

I hope this helps someone. Prove everybody that said you were stupid, ugly, and fat wrong! Remember you are Royalty! Never forget what you are worth!

Be the best you can be,

Love Chante'

I Affirm:

I love who *I am* now, *and* *I'll* always stand up for myself *and* others.

About the Author

Chante' Whisonant is 13, a Christian, and loves crocheting stuff. She has a 3-year-old cat named Katniss. She lives in Harrisburg, PA with her mom and dad. Her mother is a Prophet, and her dad is a Pastor. She has three older brothers and 1 god-sister. Chante' plans on going to the School of The Arts. Her future goal is to be a very powerful Prophet and young entrepreneur. Her likes are Vans, animals, babies, swimming, summer, clothes, making new friends, Demi Lovato, Mary Mary, Cece Winans, Austin Mahone, and Justin Bieber. Her fave colors are pink, purple, and red. She loves listening to pop, country, and sometimes hip-hop. Her dislikes are fake people, bugs, winter, rap music, and haters.

Did You Ever Stop to Think About?

Arianna M. Washington

Dear Bully,

You can't say things and expect someone to let it go by unnoticed. You also can't get away with "murdering one's spirit" because what you do will eventually catch up to you. Can't you see that? Sometimes a person just gets tired of hearing the countless whispers and feeling the judging eyes. It all becomes too much after a certain point.

You can't just decide to call someone out when they did nothing to you. Getting called a slut, faggot, and whore on a daily basis sounds like torture, doesn't it? Well you wouldn't know. You didn't experience it. You were the one starting everything! Calling people 'Satan' won't solve your problems. Calling me or anyone else mean names won't solve your problems.

In all honesty, when people say, *"Just ignore them, they'll go away,"* those are lies. If you ignore them, they'll keep trying. It's a never-ending cycle of torture and agony, while you constantly wish for things to simply, end. No more pain, no more suffering, no more rumors. You just want to wash it all away…but, the real question is: Why?

Why would you say these things, knowing that they're going to affect you in the long run, to another person, who hasn't done anything to you? Granted, some things might've been said by me, but they were unintentional and out of rage and frustration.

Talk is cheap but words will stay. Those are things that seem to define the human race. "You're not pretty enough" or, "You're not a size 0" seem to be the most popular…but sometimes, you just fail to see that the most common problems are the one's you're causing.

Saying things like, "I want to punch her in the face so bad right now," can hit a person not physically, but mentally. You can say all these things and pray that you never get caught, but in the end, it won't matter because Karma is like a boomerang. You throw it and it'll come right back, every single time, without fail.

You can say whatever you want, do whatever you please, but just know, that the things you say can impact a person more than anything else in the world. You don't know what a person is going through, they can have problems of their own, but, without fail, there's always that one, extremely dense person who can't see that.

You constantly disregard morals and common courtesy just to call another harmless individual something that doesn't even relate to them. How sad! It's a constant battle, dealing with things like that. You have some people calling you smart, beautiful, pretty, and then you have others calling you Satan, whore, slut, faggot, and many other things. It's a simple case of the bad outweighing the good.

Now that you've heard everything that needed to be said, the main question is:

How do you feel about all of this now?

Do you finally realize that words can hurt someone more than you thought?

And would you want this to be reflected onto you?

How would you feel?

You can say anything you want about someone and they might wipe the slate clean. That's what's happening now, the slate has been cleaned. You've been forgiven. You, just like everyone in the world, are human. Humans make mistakes, if mistakes weren't made, then the world would be dull and lifeless.

So all that's left to say is this:

Best of luck in life, things that have been said cannot be changed, but instead of using words to bring others down, try using them to pick someone up and see how that works out for you.

Yours truly,

The Victor, Arianna

I AFFIRM:

I, Arianna M. Washington, will vow to never devalue another person by calling them names or intentionally hurting their feelings for any reason whatsoever and I choose to always walk in *love and peace.*

ABOUT THE AUTHOR

Arianna Washington is 13 years old and lives in Houston, TX with her mom and stepdad. She has a stepsister and a dog. She loves listening to music, drawing and watching anime, and hanging out with her friends. She has hopes of traveling the world. In her words, her dream place to live would totally be Japan! Her favorite quote is by Austin Carlile, "Your uniqueness, your strength. Remember that. Don't mold yourself to others or to what others think. You're an individual. You're special."

Erasing My Hurt While Writing My Healing

De'Shaia T. Ventour

Dear Bully,

In all my years of school from elementary, to now in middle school, I have always been bullied. Do you remember how you treated me from kindergarten to second grade? Well, I'll tell you; you treated me like I was an alien because I was the only black girl in the class, and because I am dark skin. You stared at me like I was not even human. You made me feel very uncomfortable and you said weird things like, if you lick me would I taste like chocolate, and you tried to touch my hair because it wasn't straight and because it had a different texture. You saw me completely different. I struggled with my dark skin for a while. I wanted so much to be white, so I could look like everyone else and not stand out.

So I thought after we had moved out of the suburbs and I was with other black kids, I would be treated better because they are just like me. Wrong, I moved out of Wixom to Detroit in third grade, I thought I would fit in more, but the problem was that when I got there, you and some of the people started saying that I talked white, and I was told that I didn't talk or act black enough.

I was like, *how can my own kind treat me like this?* I couldn't understand why nobody liked me. So more bullying began, and continued through the years, but fifth grade was the worse.

You always bullied me for mainly my hair; it had always been natural and kinky. You had bullied me for not having straight or permed hair, and for not having a weave in my hair. I didn't always like your hair either, and to me it wasn't always cute, even though you had weaves or a perm, but I kept it to myself. You and your friends would tell me that you would love to come over my house and perm it because I needed it. You even made comments that my mama didn't know what she was doing and couldn't do my hair.

I was always by myself and didn't mess with anyone, yet you had always messed with me. And I was always the quiet, good, smart girl. Instead of following after me, doing things like me or congratulating me, you were mad and bullied me even more, trying to hurt me. You would call me a nerd and try to make me feel bad for getting good grades, and for not only answering questions in class, but being right lots of times. I like to learn. Isn't that the point of school? But when you wanted me to help you with your work or give you answers, it was OK for me to be smart, when you wanted to use me.

I think you noticed I was different from you and the other kids and that you saw me as a threat. You didn't like me because you said I thought I was better than you and the other kids. You called me a showoff, but all I want to do is be the best me, and that has nothing to do with you, unless you make it about you, because maybe you aren't even trying to be the best you.

You've smacked me, called me out of my name, tried to fight me and other things. And you knew that I didn't, and don't, like to fight, and yet you kept pushing my buttons! A group of three of you even plotted and planned to jump me the last day of school, because you didn't think you would get suspended.

Jump me, three of you!?! How fair is that, especially when all of you know that I didn't want to fight, and was even scared to fight. You told me the day before, bragging to me that you all were going to get me, even though you were just acting like my friend again just before that. I hadn't been in a fight with one girl, let alone three!

I would say that I may be scared to fight, but I was not scared of you. But you changed it around and said I was scared to fight and scared of you, when that's nowhere near true. I was scared and certainly didn't want to fight, so when I went home I told my parents.

I cried and was shaking even. I was even more confused because I just couldn't figure out what the real reason was behind why you girls didn't like me so much that you wanted to fight me.

I was going to stay home from school, but both my parents told me that I couldn't run from problems, and I had to stand up for myself. They both notified the school. My mom approached one of you on the bus the morning of the last day and told you, you better not touch me, and you said out of respect for her you wouldn't, and I was lucky.

The principal talked to us all, and it was resolved. One of you apologized, and I accepted it, but in the back of my head I was sure that I couldn't believe you. You even tried to be my friend the whole day, and the other girls left me alone. I always used to ask myself every day, why me, why did you always tease and mess with me? What did I do to you? But I figured it out, that you didn't like that I was always above you, that you couldn't stand to see me happy, and making A's, or you just had something going on in your life or house, or something had happened in your life, that since you couldn't get over, so you took all of that anger out on me since you thought I was weaker than you, that's why.

But what I can't figure out is why you teased me for my skin color when we're all black? Or for me not always knowing the latest rap music, rappers, dances, for not speaking in slang (and when I did you still teased me and said I sounded stupid) and for me not having as many name brand clothes. I mean that's just petty.

When we had a dress down day, my clothes weren't always name brand, but cute still. You would say you didn't like my clothes, but I think you thought I looked cute and just didn't want to say it, so instead, you, without me asking you or caring, gave a negative opinion about my clothes.

I or you can't help how we are born or look. You were born how you are; you weren't born flawless, you are not perfect, it's just life. See, I know why most people bully, because they are angry at something or someone, so, since they can't deal with the problem they take that anger out on other people.

But what is the reason for your bullying? (Another reason I mean). Are you trying to impress your friends or make it seem like you are the bigger, badder, stronger person? Well whatever the reason you are hiding, you are trying to make me seem like I am weaker than you, because I am the one being bullied, when you are being bullied too, just not in your friends' presence.

Did you know from you bullying me, I even bullied my sister? Yup. I was so mad that I use to come home and fight, and beat, on my sister when I really just wanted to beat on and fight you, but I couldn't because of my fear of fighting.

So because of my fear, and since I couldn't let go or let out my anger, I fought out my anger onto my younger sister, because I knew she couldn't do anything. I was turning into a bully, like you.

Do you remember when multiple times I tried to be your friend? Even after all you did to me I stilled tried, yet you still dogged me out. I do. I even started to do things that my parents didn't want me to do just to fit in and be accepted finally. You just used me and pretended to be my friend, just to bully me again.

You even said we were frenemies. Well, actually you said, *"Girl, you know we frenemies."* You said it like it was a good thing, and I should just deal with it and accept it, as if it was OK. I actually thought it was OK, not totally understanding what it meant until I talked to my mom about it, and she explained it to me, and told me I was better than that kind of relationship. She told me to not settle for less than a friend, ever, and she showed me how silly that is to be, or want to be, someone's frenemy.

You had bullied me so much that I didn't even want to go to school, and I started to have low self-esteem, and at one point in time I started disliking myself a lot, that's how bad you treated me. And that right there shows and proves that the saying, **'sticks and stones may break my bones, but words don't hurt me'** is wrong, because maybe they don't hurt physically, but mentally and emotionally they do, yes just as much as being physically hurt.

And I am one of the living examples that after all I been through, and after all you have done to me, that you can overcome your past, because it doesn't matter where you've come from, but where you are going, and what doesn't kill you makes you stronger. And that right there is the truth.

So I am going to keep on living and believing in myself and overcome any and all obstacles you and other future bullies gave/give, because I have already overcome my past and am living the present, and I'm still here, making it happen.

From the scared to now Stronger me,

De'Shaia Ventour

I Affirm:

I don't have to wear my hair, act like, think like, talk like, or dress like anyone else but me. You may not like it, but *I love* it. *I love* me; hair, skin, style, brains and all *and I am* ok with how *I am.*

About the Author

"If you put your mind to it, all things are possible," is what Native Detroiter youth, De'Shaia Ventour believes and is learning to apply to her life. She is a 12 year old honor roll student who also plays the clarinet.

Outside of school De'Shaia loves to watch TV, especially the cooking channel. She also likes to collect recipes and cook - that is when her mom allows her to. A true creator, De'Shaia also loves to sew and make her own designs, whether it is making outfits out of colorful duct tape for dolls, or sewing and designing clothes and purses for herself out of old clothes and new fabrics. De'Shaia has aspirations to go to college and become a Fashion Designer, and to own her boutique with her own fashion line.

De'Shaia Ventour is the second oldest of two sisters and a brother. She has made both her mother and father proud, and was happy that she could become an author at such a young age and be an inspiration to other young girls.

I Speak Against Bullying!

Dallas N. Thurman

Dear Bullies in the world,

Did you know that when you bully someone you are hurting yourself and the person you are bullying? Do you know that bullying is wrong? In this letter, I want to inspire you and encourage you to stop bullying.

I have never experienced being bullied before but I have seen others who were bullied, and I didn't like it. Bullying sounds, looks, and feels wrong to me. I don't like watching you bully people because when I see the victim's face, it looks very sad and offended. When I look at your face, I can see the force and evil in your actions. Watching this makes me feel sad for both of you and sometimes I feel helpless because I really don't know how to help.

When you push or shove someone in a locker, you should think about what you are doing. Have you ever asked yourself how would you feel if someone was bullying you? If you don't know what a bully is, let me tell you what the dictionary says. The word bully means "to frighten or to pick on people that are smaller and weaker than you are."

The people who are being bullied do not like being bullied. It hurts their feelings, and it affects them in many ways. They try to ignore you when you are bullying them, and they want you to stop. And when they do this, you just keep on bothering them.

One day when I was watching television, there was a young boy getting treated very badly by a group of older boys. They pushed him around and threw spitballs at him and took his toys. The young boy told his older brother, and his older brother stood up for him. The bullying stopped after that, and the young boy wasn't sad anymore. All it took was for someone to speak out and stand up to the bullies.

Do you bully people because you are sad, frustrated or hurting inside? What I don't understand is how you became a bully. Many schools have bully campaigns, and you should go to one to learn how wrong bullying is. If you let me, I will pray with you to ask God to put love in your heart and to stop the pain that's inside of you.

Do you know that love is very important in the world? God is love. His love is strong and powerful. The bible says, "We love Him because He first loved us," 1 John 4:19 KJV. If you are a bully, do you know that Jesus loves you too? All He wants is for you to stop hurting others, and this will make Him very happy.

If you don't know Jesus, He is a great person to know. He is God's son. He died on the cross for our sins. You should get to know Jesus because when you talk to him, He will give you peace and you will get to go to heaven where there is no stress. All you have to do is ask Him to come into your heart and to forgive you for all of your sins, and then He will forgive you.

Jesus loves everybody no matter what, so you should love everybody too. If you know Jesus, you should apologize to the people you hurt so they can forgive you just like Jesus did. When you ask Jesus to come into your heart, He will, and you will get to know Him better and learn how to love like Him.

To the victims of bullying,

When you are being bullied, you should ignore the person who is bullying you. If they pick on you, tell them how you feel. If the bullying is continuous, you should tell someone or stand up for yourself. Don't be afraid!

Another thing you can do to ignore bullies is to think of something good. An example of a good thing is like if you're a Christian, think of a scripture like Philippians 4:13 KJV, which says, "I can do all things through Christ who strengthens me."

If you ever get treated badly, don't retaliate! Always remember to treat people like you want to be treated. If you have Jesus in your heart, you should know that He loves everybody, and He forgives them no matter what. This means that you should do like Him and love everybody too. If a bully asks you to forgive them, do it because the same forgiveness you give to others will come back to you.

To the bystanders who have witnessed bullying,

If you have ever seen someone being bullied, I encourage you to help the victims by not standing around and just watching them be hurt or teased. You should help them by standing up for them, telling an adult or someone who can stop the bullying, or you can encourage the victim so that they can feel better about themselves.

To the parents of bullies,

If your child is a bully, stop them now! If you don't stop them now, they will remain a bully until they die.

****

Overall, bullying is wrong, and I will pray for you to learn how to love yourself and others.

Stay positive...Jesus loves you,

Dallas N. Thurman

I Affirm:

I will speak against bullying! *I will* stand up for others who are afraid to stand up for themselves! *I will* love *and* show kindness to bullies and the victims of bullying! *I will* always treat others the way that I want to be treated! *I will* pray for all people to have love in their hearts *and* to know Jesus!

About the Author

Talented, intelligent, unique, compassionate, and disciplined are just a few characteristics to describe Dallas N. Thurman.

Born on September 9, 2005 in Oak Park, Illinois, Dallas N. Thurman currently resides in her hometown of Chicago, Illinois. Although she is the only child born to her parents, Larry C. Thurman and Darriel S. Anderson, Dallas is blessed with a large loving family who is immensely supportive of her endeavors.

"Out of the mouths of babes..." is a popular scripture often quoted from the Holy Bible to depict truths and wisdom spoken by children. This scripture holds true for Dallas, whose wisdom extends far beyond her years.

When asked to describe herself, Dallas' immediate response is, "I am smart, wise, unique and talented." Thus the name Dallas, which means "wise", and Nekol means "victory of the people", which were intentionally chosen for her by both her mother and her maternal grandmother, Paris J. Anderson.

Dallas 'wisdom and compassion consistently shines through her gifts, talents, academic achievements and her service to others. She not only shines in the classroom as an "A" honor roll student, she is also a natural born leader who enjoys helping and serving others.

Dallas' hobbies include reading, writing, playing the piano, arts & crafts, dancing, and watching movies. When asked what she wants to be when she grows up, she confidently replies, "I will become a Teacher, Artist, Entrepreneur and a Philanthropist." Dallas loves God with all of her heart and she is not ashamed to share her faith and Christian beliefs with others. She regularly attends Trinity Community Baptist Church where she is an active member of the Kingdom Kids Ministry.

Expert Contribution

A Victor of Bullying

Bonetta Lynch

*I*t feels like it was yesterday that I stood at the bus stop in my neighborhood, waiting for the 7 am bus to go to my high school across town. I took it in stride, a little nervous but so excited to start a new chapter in my life.

See, this was the year that I started my first year of high school – young adulthood – more decisions, more responsibilities, academics and everything else that is part of high school that would be memorable. During those years, I encountered the pain, the hurt, the embarrassment, and the humiliation of being who I am; just me. I always wondered, during my lifetime, why was I a chosen target for such shameful scrutiny without explanation?

At the time of my experience, I knew if I did not stand firm in my own truth of not being in bondage or a victim, I would be brought into a state of constant fear. While attending school and making plans for my future, I had received confirmation from my doctor that my health had improved, and I no longer needed to wear my Milwaukee brace. Yes, freedom from 20 to 25 pounds of iron on my spine, from my neck to my torso - just the right time when starting and attending high school. Even though I felt the joy of release from the bondage of a temporary past situation, there were some individuals that made sure that what I was able to overcome, would stay a permanent fixture in my life.

There is nothing like a neighborhood bully, especially when there are two of them. It gets truly personal when the neighborhood bullies attend the same grade and middle schools where all the kids attend. Both bullies met me at different bus stops within the neighborhood to taunt, mock, and harass me as I waited each morning for the local bus. Each morning I had to go to a different location in order to get peace.

To block out the taunts, I would wear my headphones under a hat, along with a cassette player, listening to my favorite music to give me motivation. Eventually, they caught on and decided to snatch my hat off, and tried everything to disrupt my flow.

When someone constantly challenges you, you're no longer an individual. You feel like a target with nothing to fight for anymore. I was so exhausted from all of the fighting and emotional, verbal, and physical abuse from a previous bully experience, that I was practically scared into silence.

The very thought of ending it all was an option of freedom and relief, but would be absolutely pointless and would bring more shame to my family and all of those who loved me so much, but did not know the private pain that paralyzed me internally. I hoped they would have some mercy for me and my soul. It was a relief for me to watch how individuals who did not even know me fought for and supported me and made these two creeps go in complete hiding or shame.

My warfare had literally stopped when both bullies were involved in bad, violent acts, on separate occasions. One was gunned down on a hot summer day, and the other was shot twice in the head with a 365 Magnum. He was laid out in the street like a dog.

To my understanding, the gentleman who was shot in the head and laid out in the gutter amazingly lived through that ordeal. This was such a shock and unheard of in a family-oriented, middle-class community where individuals worked really hard, made preparations for the future, and basically lived their lives to the fullest. But, actually, this was real. I felt the freedom from the torment, but felt bad regarding what my bullies endured, but I knew that the healing process was about to bring a breakthrough that would be memorable. Many times, we make preparations for our lives and future, not knowing what life has in store for us.

As I reflect, I ask myself what would I do, what would I say, if I ever saw my bullies face-to-face? How would I react? Well, my curiosity had come to a true reality. My breakthrough occurred while attending a Sunday morning church "Celebration of Family and Friends Day." When celebrating, there is always lots of love, food, and people just enjoying the love of life.

While celebrating, I glanced at a gentleman in an electric wheelchair who was a quadriplegic. He had a bib around his neck and food all over the area where he had eaten. He was enjoying just being in the company of beautiful energy. As the crowd started to wind down, I heard someone call my name. Being in total amazement, this call came from the gentleman who was in the wheelchair. I replied, "Hi. How are you? How do you know my name?" He replied, "We grew up and attended the same neighborhood school together."

Totally clueless, I asked the gentleman what his name was. I never expected his reply. Something inside of me dropped like a tsunami; the gentleman in the wheelchair was my bully. It is so funny how you can rehearse over and over how you would confront your bully, and when it actually happens, you're at a loss for words. I could have really been brutal and hateful towards him, but, instead, I wept for him and embraced him.

I had to realize that God and prayer do change things for you to understand what life truly is all about. It is truly a gift to experience a breakthrough and understand my pain, my hurt, my persecution over the years. It showed me my true strength and that in spite of it all, I do have the power to do the impossible and change lives.

As a life coach, speaker, mother, and successful businesswoman, I reflect on all of the challenges I endured. I can say that there is a celebration through one's breakthrough.

Bonetta Lynch

About the Author

Bonetta Lynch, affectionately known as "The Inspirational Ignitor," has dedicated her life to inspire and motivate individuals to release their God-given talents. Diagnosed with scoliosis and neuromuscular disease, Bonetta has refused to let her disability, or society, define who she is. She has learned to live life despite her challenges, not according to someone else's standards. Armed with a deep spiritual belief in God, she uses her struggles to encourage and inspire others to live the life of their dreams to the fullest without any true potential to reach their level of destiny. As a makeup artist for 16 years and working in corporate America, she has been blessed to have the opportunity to use her creative skills in various arenas in the corporate world - fashion, video, television and film - for celebrities, political figures and social society. This accomplished businesswoman and mother has her own mobile notary service and organization called, 'Destined for Greatness New York', which caters to the special needs community. Now walking faithfully in her calling as an acclaimed author, writer, lecturer and coach, her gift and passion for life has impacted many lives through her work in many organizations such as, Autism Speaks, The Muscular Dystrophy Association, Breast and Colon Cancer, and Feeding the Homeless, just to name a few. Her biggest accomplishment and joy is being a mother of a young adult son, Christopher, who is autistic. Soon she will be receiving her biggest honor of a Bachelor's Degree in Human Service and Psychology from SUNY Empire State College.

A Mother's Fight,
A Mother's Sacrifice

Sara Dean

*I*n the eighth grade I fell in with the wrong crowd, and despite my Christian upbringing, I made some very bad choices because I wanted to fit in. When my mom found out what was going on, (I broke down and told her) she refused to let me hang out with them anymore. The next thing I knew, two of the girls I had considered such great friends before, turned on me.

They tripped me, they slammed my locker door shut on my head, they screamed mean things about me in the hallway, and they made fun of me when I ate, telling me how I should be starving myself instead of eating, even though I was skinny. I held my head high and never let on that it bothered me, but I cried every night and begged God to make it stop, which after a while, He did. But to this day I have issues with food, stemming from that time. I'm 5'7 and 127 pounds, but I exercise obsessively and watch everything I eat.

When my son started school, he was very popular everywhere he went, so I thought he make a lot of friends. But before long, he was coming home with bruises and red marks on his body, and he would get sick every day at school and call to come home. He told me that the kids would take his toys during play time, refuse to include him, and even hit him. One boy, who was supposed to be his friend, even hit him in the stomach during Music class. Despite how he was being treated, he refused to back down when he saw someone else being bullied, and the bully turned on him and twisted his arm.

I went to his teacher and then his principal. They tried to stop it, but nothing worked. After a while he began throwing up in the morning when it was time to leave. I knew something had to give, I couldn't watch him go through the same torment I did. So I prayed hard about it, and the owner of a small Christian school in our area approached me about working as a pre-school teacher and janitor at the school to work off my son and daughter's, (who was at a pre-school age) tuition. I jumped at the chance and took him out of public school.

The Christian school shut down a year later, but God had opened the doors, and the owners agreed to let the parents of their students have all of the books we needed so we could homeschool, which is what I have been doing for the last three years.

It's so hard to fit everything in with work, schooling, the kids' outside activities, church, (I help teach the nursery class there) homeschooling support group weekly, (where homeschooling children get together for activities, parties, games, and field trips) doctors/dentist/optometrist and my daughter's monthly chiropractic appointments, (she has mild scoliosis and the chiropractic appointments help with it) and babysitting my best friend's baby once or twice a week for ten hours a day while my best friend works. But I do it because I love my kids enough that I will always do whatever it takes to keep them from being bullied again.

Sara Dean

About the Author

Sara Dean lives in West Virginia with her two children, her husband, and the zoo full of animals that the kids keep bringing home. At the moment they have two dogs, four cats, a betta, a goldfish, a lion head bunny, and a corn snake named "Cornelius". Until recently, they also had four kittens and a box turtle as well.

When Sara isn't taking care of the family and pets, she is busy writing and editing. She has nearly twenty books published under her own name, including her newest series, "Where in the World is Sir Pigglesworth?" which she co-authors with Jo-Ann Wagner, and her B- Detective Agency comic book series. And she has ghostwritten over 150 books for other people. She is also the editor at Aviva Gittle Publishing and the co-owner and editor at AKW Books.

A Parent's Guide

Dr. Nicole Jones

$\mathcal{M}$y thoughts and perspectives on bullying, as well as the context, of bullying are based on five years as an elementary public school principal, eighteen years as a parent, and twenty-one years in education. As I think about how prevalent bullying is in society today, and as someone who naturally seeks ways to prevent children from developing undesirable patterns of behavior, perhaps parents can use the following three stages to deal with bullying: (a) Stage 1: Preventative Measures, (b) Stage 2: Being Present, and (c) Stage 3: Practice What You Preach.

Stage 1: Preventative Measures

If narrowed down to an age group, preventive measures should begin at birth and be reinforced daily until about eight years old (or third grade). This is a critical stage because it is the developmental stage where social and emotional behaviors are learned.

- **Teach your child empathy for inanimate objects**. This will enable them to translate that empathy to any situation at any age. For instance, if you are walking in the grass say, *"Oh, my gosh, what must that blade of grass feel like? It probably sees this big shadow coming and is screaming, 'oh no, don't crush me, don't crush me.'"* This will help the child to look at things very, very differently. The same is true for trees or any concept you use to teach them. Teach empathy from the perspective of who they harm or what is being damaged or affected.

- **Modeling care and consideration**. When doing anything, be cognizant that all eyes are on you. Just think of yourself as being under surveillance, because that is literally what your kids are doing. They are watching everything you do and processing that information for their own use at a later time.

- **Explicitly teach them by talking them through your thought process**. For example, the scenario might be that while driving, someone cuts you off. Of course, you should be very careful how you respond because the child is watching, but when you do respond, talk it out. *"Wow, that was dangerous and it scared me. My initial response may have been to blow my horn or to yell out, but would that make things better, worse, or would it help at all?"* Then say out loud, *"I think the best way for me to deal with this situation is to be thankful that nobody was hurt. I also wonder what caused that person to do what they did."*
If you are able to speculate, tell the child and talk about it (maybe you saw them texting, putting on makeup or being distracted). Then go deeper and include yourself. *"I have to be careful, too, if I use those things while driving because I have to be cautious about the cars around me. Better yet, I should not do those things at all because now I see what can happen."* Talk them through *your* thought process so it helps them develop their own thought processes.

- **Teach the value of authority figures**. Help the child understand that an authority figure is entrusted with their care. Sometime, as parents, we tell our kids, *"don't lie to me and your father"* or *"make sure you* *do what I tell you to do,"* etc. These statements can sometimes send mixed signals. Is the child supposed to do what a trusted adult tells them to do or just what their parents tell them to do? Are they supposed to respond only to mom or dad?

They may fail to recognize who they can trust because parents may not always be around. Later in life, you may want them to trust a police officer, a school counselor, the person who is over the dorm in college, or you may want them to go to internal affairs in their business/workplace. You want to talk about authority figures so that they understand that in every aspect of life there is a trusted person to whom they can go for help.

Replace *I* and *me* with a trusted authority figure. Teach them to ask their teacher, babysitter, or pediatrician for help/guidance so that they understand there is always someone around that they can talk to even if it is not you, the parent. You really want to put them in a situation where they can trust an adult because as they get older, they will start to look to others—the Internet and friends—to make decisions. One should start early to show that there are people around that are wise and can be trusted.

- **Broach difficult subjects early**. This shows that you are open and receptive. You want to your kids to realize that they can come to you about anything, so you can't be afraid of discussing certain subjects. It is never too early to talk about difficult subjects. If you and your child witness anyone making a poor choice, you need to say something immediately.

For instance, you may see Auntie do something inappropriate. Your response could be, *"Hey, Auntie got really upset and if she had had the time, she would have handled that differently."* The child may think they are too young to talk about this type of behavior, but say to them you are not talking about Auntie but addressing the behavior. Use that situation as a teachable moment. Remind your children that as the parent, you may talk about things that appear to them to be off limits. However, let them know that what they may perceive to be an inappropriate topic, may, in fact, be a timely and necessary discussion to have. There will be occasions where they will have a voice in what is going on around them, but as the parent your decisions are final. This allows you to talk about how you perceive the situation and how you would react.

- **Provide your child with diversity**. Design your life with as much diversity as possible, inclusive of economics, gender, ethnicity, race, religion, and family structure. In doing so, you allow your children to understand that people are unique and different, and that there is no one way of seeing and doing anything. They will learn that people have different shapes, sizes, backgrounds, and cultures. When children see differences on a daily basis, they are less prone to bully and hurt others later in life.

- **Teach your child not to judge or make assumptions about others.** Have a conversation with your child about the homeless and people with physical or mental disabilities. Unfortunately, people sometime bully those who fall into these categories. If your child makes statements about other people's frailties, use this opportunity to ask them how they think the person came to be in this situation or circumstance.

As parents, we have to talk through those things that we may want to ignore because we do not know if and how to discuss them. However, it is important that you continue to build that foundation for empathy and to have your child understand that life is about a lot of different people and a lot of different situations.

- **Teach your child about relationship building**. From the moment they are born, emphasize sharing, compromising, listening, and thinking before speaking. When I was pregnant with my third child, her siblings were five and seven years old and not comfortable with the expected addition to our family. We talked about how she doesn't know anyone, but the two of you know each other.

  This can translate to the new kid sitting in the lunchroom alone or the person in your study group in college who just does not seem to fit. Being the new kid on the block is no fun. Teach your child to be accepting and empathetic to people who appear to need a friend.

- **Get the child's opinion about everything**. In the framework of a democracy, everyone has a voice but children must understand that their choices are limited. The child will begin to feel empowered knowing that he/she can make decisions, that opinions are valued, and the feelings they express mean something.

  For instance, when shopping for cereal, give them the option of choosing among brand A, brand B, and brand C, brands that you have selected. You have just narrowed their choices so that they are safe and healthy but the child feels empowered because he/she was able to choose. You want children to feel that they can be vocal, that their opinions matter and that you value their opinion; otherwise, when they get older they will be less likely to say how they feel.

Start young and start now so you can squash negative feelings from within. This also helps children to realize their power when it comes to relationships and in this case, bullying.

- **Build self-esteem**. False self-esteem is expressed when people always say they are great and clap for every little thing they do. Push children into areas where they will excel and have an inclination or propensity to be successful, like a sport. If you see that your child is really good with critical thinking skills, expose them to ways that would help them feel validated in those areas, like chess or board games. If they have really good hand-eye coordination, get them into sports. In sports, they learn to trust authority figures, sportsmanship, healthy competition, and how to stay fit and active.

  But, even more than that, look at their inclination. If they are beating on things, introduce them to an instrument. If there is a strong desire to color and paint, let them do that and introduce them to the various arts. The formative years are about exposing children to as many learning opportunities as possible. They are trying to find themselves and their gift(s). You have to help them discover their talents because it all makes them stronger individuals with high self-esteem.

- **Teach the importance of expressing feelings**. Parents have to model this practice by not lying to friends and family. Our lives are very intertwined with our children and they are watching our every move, picking up on what you do and don't do, and how you do it even when you think they are not paying attention or are distracted by their own activities. They are always listening even when you think they are asleep, reading, listening to music with headphones, doing homework, or in the car.

So if you don't want to go to grandma's house, don't lie about it. Say mom, dad, we love you and we know you want to see us. I am sure you made a great meal but I am so exhausted. I just really want to get the kids home, give them a bath, and rest a bit. Once off the phone, explain to the kids how that was tough to do but it has been hard day. Hopefully we can make it up to them by visiting them on another day. This way you are showing empathy but also you are being steadfast in how you feel about certain things and you say it without hurting anyone's feelings.

- **Be active in their lives**. Join the PTA, the recreational center, or swim team. You need to survey what is going on and get to know the people that are involved. Ask yourself the following questions: (a) Does this feel like an environment that empowers children? (b) Does this feel like a team where the coach is not as obsessed with winning as with teaching the children hard work, preparation, value, and doing your best? In order to build the right foundation, work your hardest at this stage to set them up in an environment where they feel valued, where they will be exposed to those character traits that you believe to be positive and the best fit for your child. Immerse them in opportunities that should result in them feeling empowered, in control, self-assured, self-aware, and empathetic.

Stage 2: Being Present

Stage 2 concentrates on nine-twelve year olds, from fourth to eighth grade. I have worked in schools where 99% of the children qualify for free and reduced lunch to schools where only 2% qualify for free and reduced lunch. No matter where, there is just something about fourth grade where children start to realize alliances. Kids begin to realize that they have choices about people with whom they want to be aligned. The children make birthday and slumber party lists in class and show them to those who are not invited.

All of the values they were taught in their formative years now come into play. However, you have to be present to analyze what you have taught them with what is happening around and to them. Also, pay attention to the personality and identity that your child is developing.

- **Help your children define the differences between teasing and bullying because they are very different**. There is also a difference between being assertive and being aggressive. As parents, we have to define those differences accurately, discuss them fully, and redirect them as much as possible. Teasing, once it becomes offensive, not liked, results in hurt feelings or embarrassment, turns into bullying. If mean comments are being made (i.e., racial or sexually explicit comments) and they are met with laughter, you are not being bullied or harassed. If immediately after such comments, it is stated that there was an offense taken, the very next time similar comments are made, it is harassment and/or bullying.

- **Teach them to set boundaries**. These are the same boundaries that you have taught them in the formative years. These are the instincts that you have taught them to say, feel, and trust.

- **Teach them to verbalize their wants and desires**. Children tend to state things and not positions. An example is a child stating that their homework is hard or that someone is mean. That doesn't really state their position. You have to teach them to rephrase and say I need help with my homework or tell the person bothering them to stop talking about them because it hurts their feelings or they just don't like it. As parents, we have to get our children to take a position in situations when things happen to them. This can be very hard but this is where you have to build confidence.

- **Define good friendship behavior**. When I am working with children and they have disagreements like he/she bothers me or he/she bullies me, I talk to them one-on-one and simply say, *"Let's list the characteristics of a good friend and put your friend's name on the other side."* Then, I have them check off all of those behaviors that they value to see if their friend has those same characteristics.

  When done this way, the child is shown that the other child is not a bad person but just does not have the character traits that are valued in a friend. After the child sees that, you can move on to a friend that has those character traits. You can ask who they know that is kind and who has the other qualities that they value and look for in a friend.

Be careful not to preach to children——*"I told you not to be with her! I told you to stay away from her!"* None of that works. There is something about that person that they like or find fascinating whether the other child is popular, smart, or dresses nicely. Whatever the case may be, that is why they have decided to align themselves with that individual. So, then you have to go back to the characteristics of a friend, stating that she/he may be all of that (popular, dresses nicely, smart, etc.) but do they treat you with respect, say kind words to you, do they influence or set the example for others to treat you with respect, or do they encourage others to be friends with you? Your child knows what friends are supposed to look like because they read books and watch movies; so let them write it out so they can see for themselves.

You can then compare the lists of traits with them by asking if this a true friend and a friend that they would want to have in their life. By doing this, you're setting the stage for dating, marriage, and for an environment that is supportive and nurturing.

- **Manufacture opportunities**. Give children a chance to meet with other children that you believe have families like yours and think/operate like yours. If you have friends or people you know who have children around the same age and they have similar values as you, try to arrange to have everyone get together, but listen to your child. Kids have great instincts. If they say that they are not interested and they don't want to go, don't push it. Try instead to arrange play dates.

Play dates allow you choose an environment that you believe will be supportive of them. When my children were younger and I was not sure how they would interact with other kids, I would monitor, listen, drop in, and engage in conversation. As children get older, you have to be present and help navigate situations. So have play dates and encourage relationships. Their first relationship is with family, the second is with friends, which leads to relationships at work and with mates. How well we navigate relationships— listening, thinking, and compromising—will impact how successful we are in life.

Stage 3: Practicing What You Preach

This stage includes thirteen-year-olds to adults. When we were children, our parents or guardians instilled in us the values they believed to be right. They were our role models. If they asked you to do something, more than likely they did it, too. As parents, we must continue to practice what we preach and trust that all of the time invested in our children's developmental stage (birth to eight years old) will result in a well-rounded, emotionally stable human being.

- **Investigate everything.** When dealing with bullying, nothing is as it seems. Don't walk up into the school, on campus, or on the coach and be a bully yourself. Emotions can become heightened when one believes that your baby has been hurt in some way. That mama bear, parental instinct kicks in and you go in angry with demands and assumptions. It is important that you model the correct behavior—go and see what has happened, talk to the person in charge, and investigate.

  Sometimes things are not what they seem. As a principal, I have investigated complaints of bullying from parents. However, when I talked to the source or the teacher, sometimes I found that both children were at fault. Sometimes there is a real case of bullying going on, but you want to go in with an open mind so that there is the possibility of working together with the administration to solve the problem.

- **Assume goodwill**. Children are only the best that they know how to be sometimes. Many times you may interact with parents or guardians and it becomes very apparent from whom the children have gotten those behaviors or where they may have seen those behaviors. This is the time to utilize the adults that are your resources and talk through the problem with the child.

In conversations that I have had with parents, I never devalue a parent or what they bring to the table. One of the most frequent responses I hear from children is that their parent said if someone hits them, then they are to hit them back.

My response is that that sounds like a very valuable mom and/or dad rule at home, but now you're at school and we have school rules and we can't hit. I explain to parents why students can't hit each other and explain to them that times are different from back in the day when once a child hit another and they hit back, they were done fighting and it was over.

That isn't the case anymore. There is a big brother, an uncle, or a parent ready to come to the school and take action against what has happened to their relative. In some cases, parents go to the person's house to confront the child or the parent of the child. Because of this kind of scenario, things can get out of hand really easily, and we have to expect the unexpected. Even after the children have moved past the incident, the families are still engrossed in what has occurred and it becomes a huge mess.

These unfortunate outcomes could have been avoided if the resources available to parents would have been utilized. Therefore, I say assume goodwill first and talk it through because children tend to act like those around them. These negative behaviors sets the child up for a world of failure and it can also endanger them because it can draw in other people.

- **Know your rights and investigate your rights**. Before talking to someone at school about bullying, pull up the school's policy and see what it says so you know your options. Options should be solution-oriented. Children can't be sent home if one day they have behavioral problems. They are in school to learn and sometimes that continuous learning does not occur in the home. Children become immersed in everything that is happening around them and they have to sort out what is appropriate from what is being done at school and what is being done at home. Sometimes they have to start from ground zero everyday when they walk back into the classroom.

But again, you have to be solution-oriented and know what the policies are. Understand that you can ask for a meeting with the other parent or have the administrator or teacher do a sit down with the parent and you may be able to request that the other child who is bullying be included. You can sign contracts and agreements about expectations based on school policies; schools usually have policies that cover first, second, and third offenses. You must know your rights and what you have in your power to do. You may even suggest that the other child gets counseling if things persist because, again, we are talking about children and we want to help all of them.

In cases where the teacher may be missing or not paying attention to what is going on in class, especially among girls because their type of bullying isn't always as obvious as boys, you can talk to the teacher and make them aware of what is happening in the classroom. Have your child be vocal on what is going on as well. You have to get the teacher to understand the importance of the matter and how this all makes for a hostile environment for your child.

The administrator of the school has leeway lots of time on how stuff is handled. Remember that the school can only share information about your child; they can't go into detail about the outcomes of the other child. This doesn't mean that the school is holding back or that nothing is being done. It means that the school is working through the process and is honoring the rights of everyone involved, including your child.

- **Set timeframes and time constraints**. You can set reasonable timeframes as to when situations should be investigated and handled, and you can follow up on everything and get answers on your end on how to move forward.

- **Document events/results and keep your proof of bullying is possible**. Always keep documentation of what is going on and have proof of what has transpired (keeping bullying texts, cyber bullying posts, any letters of communication that you have written, dates, etc.) and the results that come from each instance.

- **Follow your instincts**. If a determination is made and it just doesn't make sense to you, trust your instincts. There is a hierarchy and you can go to the teacher, to the counselor, to the assistant principal, to the principal, or to the area director of that particular school. You can also talk to personnel in other areas such as the coach, assistant coach, the director over the recreational center, etc. Make sure that you follow the hierarchy first because trying to go straight to the superintendent will only delay action, but don't stop if you don't feel validated.

  In a healthy environment where all processes are being followed or enforced, no one take offense to you going to a higher authority. A statement indicating that you are not comfortable with a decision can move you to the next step.

  You have to do whatever is necessary for your child because sometimes people will overlook things in the investigation—don't get truthful information, don't have enough witnesses, and whatever the case may be. So continue to be an advocate for your child.

- **Follow through**. Always stay connected and involved so that you protect your child. Don't let up. You have to feel comfortable that you are sending your child somewhere safe emotionally and physically. That is your right to go after and implement that want and desire.

****

In conclusion, dealing with bullying and combativeness comes in three stages. The preventive stage is where you work your hardest to create a child that has the self-esteem and the confidence that they will need to navigate the world that they will eventually inherit. Children see and learn the power of behavior based on how you demonstrate and teach them to behave.

The second stage is where you have to be present. It is literally when you begin to synthesize what you have taught them with what is happening to them and around them in the world.

The final stage is where you have to be pragmatic and practice what you have taught them. At this stage, if something happens that needs your attention, you have to act within those boundaries you taught them so that you get the outcome in which you both feel safe.

Our first experience with the microcosm of society will impact how we handle our relationships and every organization within society. Parenting is a huge factor that determines if a child will be a bully or will be bullied.

Dr. Nicole Jones

About the Contributor

Nicole Evans Jones is a native of Atlanta and is the proud mother of three children currently enrolled in middle school, high school, and college.

As a school administrator, Nicole provides vision and leadership for the instructional program. In doing so, Nicole organizes the implementation and monitoring of a system of teaching and learning that focuses on the following five areas: school climate, knowledge of content, student engagement, instructional rigor, and relevance, and assessment strategies and usage. Over Nicole's twenty year career as an educator, she has served as an assistant principal, instructional liaison, and a counselor in both urban and suburban school settings.

Nicole holds a Bachelor of Arts degree in Political Science from Howard University, a Master of Arts degree in Counseling and Human Growth and Development from Clark Atlanta University, and a Doctorate of Education in Educational Leadership from Clark Atlanta University. Nicole is a graduate of the 2010 Summer Leadership Institute at Harvard University, where she also participated on a principal panel and presented to educators from around the world.

It Takes a Village
to
Take a Stand against Bullying

Anita Fendall

We don't birth bullies. Bullying is a learned behavior that is being picked up by or exposed to the child somehow, whether in the home or around those they hang around with.

In a perfect world, bullying can be completely eliminated. Although we do not live in a perfect world, something can be done about bullying. Even though it starts with the parents, it is more than just the parents, and it is more than just a teacher. It takes the collective to decrease bullying around us.

What Can Parents Do?

My husband and I actually went through bullying with our two children. Our daughter was very vocal about her bullying, but our son didn't say anything, and we didn't find out until years later after the fact. But as parents, just like we did with our daughter, we showed him love, support, and built their confidence. EVERDAY we told our daughter she is beautiful, you're special, I love you, etc. Even now, daily we tell them that we love them. So when they come up against the negative acts of others, they have enough support and love from family to strengthen them. Be there for them by supporting, loving, empowering, and encouraging your child.

We also kept them in different activities, like church, and different environments outside of school where they could have and make true friends. We knew the kids and their parents that they hung around within our neighborhoods. That way, if anything went wrong between them, all of the parents could discuss it.

Parents play an important role that empowers their children to give them the stability and foundation that they need. Keep them busy in various activities and environments. This will also help them forge relationships with different kids outside of school.

Cyber bullying is increasing more than ever with the growth and availability of the Internet, social media, and technology. It needs to be addressed at a very early age for all children. Parents should know what their children are doing, (or what is being done to them), whether they suspect that their child is being bullied or not, or is a bully or not.

Kids are usually given phones, laptops, tablets, etc. without any boundaries. It is a just "here you go" type of situation, and that is it. We have to talk to our kids. Help them to be conscious of what they are doing before they hit that send button because it can never be retracted, regardless if it is deleted on their end. You don't want your child to take part of cyber bullying, initiate cyber bullying, or put themselves in a position that could lead to cyber bullying.

A suggestion for parents is contracts. I have agreements that I give to parents for their children that states the boundaries on how to conduct themselves online, phone, or whatever technological devices/social media/Internet sites, are being used. If broken, by using any devices or accounts/profiles in a negative way, then privileges are lost. It should be explained that the contract is beyond just stating rules and restriction but to provide and ensure safety for their well-being. Everyone should read through it together, have a complete understanding, and sign one of these. Dependent on the terms set (time, usage) may need to revise as your child ages, grades change, become more involved in after school activities, etc.

Check your child's social media account, email, video games, phone activity, including text messages, pictures, etc often (renew passwords as well, to prevent hacking). If parents want to know what their children's online activities are, another suggestion is to Google your kids name and sees what comes up. Your child's activity will come up and what social media accounts and Internet interactions that they have, and you can see any cries for help and/or inappropriate behavior/pictures/posts, and sharing/encouraging things you may deem unacceptable.

Parents:

- Online or offline, set boundaries for their children.
- Respond immediately if they become aware of abnormal or inappropriate behavior.
- Get help for your children.
- Pay attention and look for signs, obvious and not so obvious.

What Can Schools Do?

When bullying arises, schools (teacher, principals, and staff) should be able to take the proper actions and precautions, because a child cannot effectively deal with bullying alone. Most school systems do not have enough staff or manpower to do what needs to be done to help prevent bullying. They are not equipped to handle and diffuse bullying fully but have to still do their best to ensure the safety and quality of learning within school.

Schools have to empower those that are being bullied. Students should feel safe and should not stay victimized when trying to get an education. Get their input too, in addition to the teacher and parent. Most times kids do not feel comfortable with what is going on and have no say in it either, which can make them even more insecure. Let them become more involved in coming up with a solution to the problem by forming a plan with them that they feel comfortable with.

When I work within the school systems I advise schools to come up with different, but effective, tactics to help the child being bullied in addition to detention, suspension or being kicked out of school. We say the word, 'bully' but it is about their actions that we also need to focus on outside of the label. Bullies show a lot of potentially great characteristics, but it is just filtered in a negative way. If schools can learn to work with a child that demonstrates bullying behavior and take that negative behavior and use it in a positive way that would help the bully as well.

They have great leadership skills, are very creative, and are very influential. They can get other kids to follow them with whatever negative tactics they use to achieve a goal. So if they were able to be over something (like being a classroom project or assignment, something that involves being a leader) that would take those negative leadership skills and turn them into positive leadership skills. There is obviously something going on with the child, and they are acting out trying to get the attention of others.

In addition, in a perfect world it would be great to integrate and teach empathy, acceptance, and respect within the schools for all students and sometimes for the staff as well.

Schools:

- Walk your talk by implementing the policy that is set in place, don't let it just be a written paper that has no meaning or relevance when a real situation comes about. May also include revising the policy to help recreate a striving school culture.

- Be active in trying to prevent and speak out against bullying, beyond just having posters on the wall.

- Find out where the hotspots are (usually unsupervised or hidden areas) inside and outside of school where bullying can/does occur and have the area supervised (bathrooms, hallways, back of the building etc).

- Follow through, and follow up, and always communicate, seeing it through to the end.

What Can the Community Do?

I am old school, real old school, and I always say we need to come back to the front porch. Nowadays we are blessed to have people that work from home, retirees, etc. who can become active in what is going on with our kids within the community.

Many times bullying occurs when there are no adults around. We have to go the extra mile and do what our neighbors and communities use to do back in the day. Once, I saw a group of kids gathering around because two kids were about to fight. I stopped my truck to see what was going on. I didn't know these kids, but I knew they were up to no good. It was a dangerous thing for me to do, and I had no idea what I was up against, but I made them all go home.

We need to come back and be more active in our kids' lives, showing love and concern, and being more vigilant in helping one another. If we begin to take notice and watch kids when there is no supervision, like when they walk home from school or when the school busses come and leave, start coming outside and observing, it could help. Also establishing this neighborhood watch will make kids think twice if they know someone is not only watching but will take action against wrongdoing. Local businesses within the neighborhoods can also get involved and offer support.

Communities:

- Pay attention to when kids begin to gather around
- Intervene, get help, say something; just do something!
- Work together and genuinely be there for each other.
- Communicate with each other and even the kids, get to know them and reestablish that community alliance among within the neighborhoods and surrounding areas.

What Can a Person being Bullied Do?

To stand up for yourself, you have to begin with you. First things first, it is all about how you, the person being bullied, feel about themselves. You have to carry yourself in a way that a person who would normally bully you, wouldn't bully you, because everything in you shows confidence.

A bully doesn't pick on someone who is strong-willed, walks upright, not slumped or slouched down, and carries themselves in a very positive way. They look for people that are weak, or who they perceive to be weak, someone they can overpower. You have to be confident. In doing so, a bully will think twice before they trying to attack you because they will think you may be able to defend yourself. Even if the bully does attempt something, stay strong in your position, and maintain full eye contact. Even if you are being bullied, (because in many cases the bullying is already taking place and the person being bullied is struggling with their confidence) your confidence can and is building slowly, it may not happen overnight, but the bully will begin to see the change and shift in you and that you are not the same person, and they will begin to stray away from you.

You have to show that inner confidence and beauty in the inside (beauty isn't just on the outside, it is within.) This includes the child who may be considered overweight, may not have the "nice" clothes, or any outer "imperfection". If you have confidence, regardless of what you look like, that will change the dynamics of everything with you and others. I have seen cases where children bullied others because they didn't have what the others had. Lots of times a child that is bullied turns into a bully, and this was one of those cases where it was a defense mode.

So it isn't about the other, regardless of what you do or don't have, it is about the inner person and it is the inner person that shows outwards, and depending on what you are outwardly showing, is what will attract the bully. We all want to project confidence, real confidence.

Bullied:

- Portray confidence in the way that you walk and talk
- Make eye contact
- Hold your head up high
- Project (not loudly) your voice

- Don't be scared to be yourself

What Can the Bully Do?

Bullies can suffer from low self-esteem and confidence as well, but I believe the main issue that causes them to lash out, and this is what the bully has to realize, is that something is missing in their life. The first step is realizing that, the next step is trying to find what that is, but you can't do it alone.

Bullies:

- Make the decision to change
- Journal or some other productive/active way as to vent and have a release
- Think before acting
- Be willing to talk through what you are feeling and experiencing, more than lashing out in response to what you are going through and be honest. Seek help, most importantly.
  - Talk to your parent (If you can't, confide in a teacher, family member, or another adult).
  - Get counseling.
  - Get a mentor

What Can Bystanders Do?

Maybe you are not a bully or have never been bullied, but wonder if there is something you can do, or should you even do anything, when you witness bullying. Of course, I think there should be advocates for those being bullied. Those who speak out against bullying are called bystanders, and they are a part of the 3B's, the bully, the bystander, and the person being bullied. The bystander has so much more power than they realize.

Being an advocate shows the bully that bullying is not right, and not the avenue they want to go down. It demonstrates to the bully as well what is acceptable, not just to show them they are wrong but to show them the way by example. A bystander has the advantage of playing the middle ground. You can go to the bully and say hey, this person is cool, or this person didn't do anything to you. You can befriend the person that is being bullied as well, so they won't feel so alone and isolated. You can help alleviate judgment and opinions from others about the person being bullied; maybe even the bully as well.

Now I don't always recommend or advise the bystander to directly intervene during the bullying at that moment. This is because a lot of times the person who is bullying may even turn on the bystander, which can escalate things to another level.

Bystanders:

- Go get help. Find an adult to tell.
- Do not stand around because bullies usually want an audience. If there isn't anyone there to perform in front of or for, then chances are they won't perform.
- Recognize your power and use it to create change around you.

In Closing:

We need programs that are geared towards helping, teaching, empowering adults with these issues just as much as we need programs geared towards our children. Adults have the ability to change things and should unite together.

Our children are stronger than they realize and regardless of what side of the spectrum they are on, they need our guidance, support, example and our advocacy.

As a collective effort we can put a big dent in bullying. It takes a village to raise a child, starting from the home, the schools, community, and everyone around if we all willing work together.

Anita Fendall
Founder of Tease Free Kids

About the Contributor

Anita Fendall is the founder of Tease Free Kids, Anti-Bullying and Leadership Speaker, Consultant and Author. As a mom of four, she has witnessed and observed the effects of bullying within the school system and the community. The peer pressure and after effects of being teased, bullied, or picked on, reduces a child's ability to be a confident and productive citizen. That is why she is on this mission to eliminate and prevent bullying for the next generation, and to rehabilitate both the bully and the victim lives.

She specializes in anti-bullying and leadership presentations. Anita challenges her audience to realize that the change starts at home, continues in the school, and is birthed into the community. www.teasefreekids.com

Getting to the Root of the Issue

Juanita Tookes. MA, TLLP

Sharisa T. Robertson:

What is bullying? I ask because the term in some cases may not be bullying but because it is heard and seen so much, we may mislabel what bullying is.

Juanita Tookes:

In my opinion, bullying is a form of aggressive behavior. Typically in all cases it is unwanted aggressive behavior, amongst school age children. Typically it starts in elementary school all the way up to high school, and it involves either a real, or perceived, concept of power or some imbalance between two individuals or groups of individuals. So there is clearly someone who feels inferior to someone else, and then there is somebody feeling superior to someone else.

Sharisa T. Robertson:

Is bullying a reflection of parents and/or something going on within the household? Same with when a child is being bullied, is that, too, a reflection of the victim's household as to why they are bullied, i.e. lack of confidence?

Juanita Tookes:

That's a good question. I do think bullying does reflect the home environment.

As far as the aggressor, or the person who is doing the bullying, it could reflect something that they see in their house. Maybe between their parents; they see how their parents handle different issues either physically or verbally abusive. They may reflect that in their school environment.

Another reason could be witnessing interactions that go on in the household and maybe their child is dealing with different emotions from seeing that. So let's just say that there is physical and verbal abuse among the child's parents. That is difficult for a child to understand and interpret. It looks like a very painful type of picture. Children in that regard feel helpless, you know, "I can't help my mom. I see my dad jumping on my mom. I am scared, and I can't help her, and she's getting hurt."

Because they feel helpless within their home, when they get to school there is this persona; "*That just because I am helpless at home, I am not about to be helpless in school. So people around here are about to know that I mean business. People are about to be scared of me. Because when I am at home my mom is scared of my dad, and there is nothing I can do there. But if people are scared of me, I can control people here.*" So it gives the child a sense of power to counteract the sense of helplessness that may be reflected within the home.

In that same token, that person who is being bullied, it may or may not reflect their home environment. I was bullied too in middle school and for me, it didn't necessarily reflect my home environment, but at the same time, when I was getting bullied I wasn't confident enough to talk to my parents about the bullying, because I didn't know exactly what they were going to do. My parent's reaction would probably be to go up to the school, and I didn't want that because that would make it worse. My mom could come up to the school today, but tomorrow I would still have to see these people. So I didn't want my mom's innate reaction to make things worse for me.

So I think for the person being bullied there is just a fear that if the situation is handled by the adults, it is just going to make the bullying even worse. Which is why I think a lot of kids keep that in, they don't want to be looked at as a tattle tell. They don't want to be looked at as weak. They don't want to endure more bullying, but ironically they do. Even when they don't say anything to an adult they still incur more bullying, they are still perceived as weak and helpless.

I think with that, there comes a lack of identity and strength if the person is being bullied. When you know who you are and have a strong concept of self, there is a lot of things you will not allow. But a lot of times parents don't invest that strong sense of self-identity into their children. So they go to school trying to be identified by cliques of popular people, and try to be accepted, and when they are rejected, that is kind of when the bullying has a place to feed, when you have rejection and feel like an outcast.

But even in school myself, I have seen individuals who were not in a clique and who were not accepted, and they were fine with it. They held their own.

As human beings, we all want to be accepted as a part of a bigger group. But there have been a few individuals that I have seen growing up who was not part of a bigger group, and they didn't seem to have a problem with that.

I do think these are both very important factors related to the home environment that is expressed in the aggressor, the bully, and the one who is getting bullied.

Sharisa T. Robertson:

How does girl on girl bullying differ from boy on boy bullying?

Juanita Tookes:

The reasoning may be a little bit different. So as far as girl on girl bullying, which is what I endured, I think it is such an environment of comparison and cattiness to be honest with you. Comparison, in that…when I was bullied, the group of girls who were bullying me, they had a more expensive brand name clothes, flashy jewelry, it was actually kind of excessive for kids at that age and in that grade.

Now that I am older, and I am studying human behavior, I now can kind of see that it is a way of overcompensating what they lack on the inside. That is the foundation of bullying, lacking something, either something in your environment, home, self, school, something is not adding all the way up. Because of being frustrated with that, they take it out on somebody else. And that is for both girl on girl bullying and boy on boy bullying.

With females, it is more of a popularity contest type of thing, just showing their exterior, like clothes and making fun of people who don't look like them. Trying to showcase, "That my outward appearance is way more important that what you are on the inside."

So a possible scenario would be that I have all of the flashy clothes, hair, etc., and you're very smart. Now I want to be smart and my grades may not be as good as yours. But through this bullying, I am showing that I am upset that I can't quite grasp the academics like you can, so I am going to make it very un-cool to be smart. So I am going to pick on you and call you nerd. Then I am going to make fun of your clothes and your glasses. I am going to have you be my flunky and get my books out of my locker, because I am going to show this whole entire school that being smart is un-cool, but being flashy is very cool. Because I am trying to compensate for the fact that I would really like to be smart but I just don't know how to ask for help because it makes me feel embarrassed.

A lot of times, one of the areas I have been working in for the last nine months of so, is behavior issues. Lots of times, children will act out behaviorally because it is tied to difficult emotions that they can't quite express, or explain to adults, like embarrassment. Embarrassment is a very difficult experience for a child to admit to or even understand within themselves. "I am embarrassed because I am not quite as smart as you! But I don't want to admit that or even know how to explain it, so I am going to act it out."

As far as boys go, it is kind of like a power trip type of thing. And this is even seen with animals, with males trying to prove their dominance with a particular species or in mating, etc. Even when a boy is younger, doing all these rough displays just to show I can hang tough with everyone else. I still do think there is that foundation of overcompensating for something they don't have. But I think more so with the boys it isn't necessarily on how I look, compared to how you look. It isn't about looks. It is about power. Showing that they can carry some power where they are at. That can tie back, like I said, to the home environment where they feel helpless or inferior at home, but try to prove to be the boss man at school and over others.

In general, I think it is more so about power and control. With girls, it is more so about outer looks and comparison between other girls.

Sharisa T. Robertson:

Good stuff. So this sparks a question. What about the girl that is bullying, but she is very smart, but she may be, I guess scared to show it. Is that her being maybe jealous of the girl who is comfortable in her intellect?

Juanita Tookes:

That is a good question. There are some smart bullies too. All bullies do not lack in academics or knowledge. I think any individual who is scared to show their intelligence has been shown a bad outcome, as a result. One of the theories of psychology is that a lot of behavior is operant conditioning, whereas a behavior is performed, and it is coupled with reinforcement or lack of reinforcement.

So if being intelligent made you popular, with being popular being the reinforcer, then there would be no fear in showing how smart one is. But if showing intelligence gives a negative response, like being called a nerd, then there would be hesitation participating fully in school to avoid enduring anything negative.

I think the basic foundation is that if a bully who is intelligent is choosing not to show their intelligence, and in fact makes fun of someone else for showing theirs, I believe they experience an interaction where they did feel comfortable at one point, but it was coupled with a negative response. So that has placed a fear in them to never try that again, and anybody who is comfortable, they are going to pick on them because they wish they could be in that same comfort level as the other person, but they are in fact, too scared to be. But they in return make that person scared of them, so that person can feel how they feel, hoping to make them feel uncomfortable showing their intelligence, because misery loves company.

Sharisa T. Robertson:

Are our girls more aggressive these days in your opinion? And is bullying, as a whole, worse in this generation from past generations, or is just more amplified because now it is on the news, and we can even witness it on social media?

Juanita Tookes:

I think bullying is worse now than before, especially when I was coming up in school, and that is because of…you said it, social media. Social media wasn't a factor at all for us. Now kids have access to social media as early as elementary school age. I didn't get on Facebook until my freshman year in college. I went through elementary, middle school, and high school with nothing. I had a cell phone, but all you could do was text.

Quite frankly, to be honest, I miss those times when I wasn't bombarded with everyone else's thoughts and business. Because the bad part of social media is all that we are doing is reading words and seeing pictures, and what we read is left up to interpretation depending on who is reading it. People look at things in different ways, so when people post statuses and try to do the subliminal attacks it can lead to cyber bullying thanks to social media.

Now we have social media, and I think technology is great, very helpful, informative, and innovative, but it also has its downsides, just as there are downsides to not having the technology, like being able to talk to people across country, connecting with family, schoolmates, friends, etc. At the same time though, social media has such a heavy reign on how people behave. It is interesting how social media and the Internet control behavior because the images that these kids are seeing, is causing such an impact to mimic them in real life. For example, I just saw a child a few weeks ago who was scared to go to sleep because they saw a very scary character that was made up on the Internet, for the Internet, with the intent to scare. **(Character name and details were purposely left off to not encourage or promote kids looking it up.)**

So we worked for months to get him to sleep on his own without his parents, and it was successful until he saw this image. I did my research on this character, and it is very scary looking. It is mind baffling that someone made up this character with these cruel and sick intentions and motives. We have children as young as eight and nine on the Internet, maybe even younger. There were some girls who were recently charged because they were trying to inflict the same pain on their friend as this character did on its victim. These girls were fourteen and are now facing adult charges.

Another problem is guns; kids were not bringing guns to school when I was a child. Of course guns were in existence, but we didn't see any school shootings. If there was, it was very rare and if it did occur it was more than likely in high school not elementary school. Now we have this whole pattern of school shootings from elementary school all the way to college. That was a pattern for a long time. It seemed like it was happening so often, around the same time, with multiple people hurt and fatalities being reported.

I do believe as the times are changing and we are becoming a more technical age, is also feeding into this bullying, because of the easy access to images and resources that children get a hold, of and bring into their learning environment that then brings negative behavior into the school. Again with guns, they see what guns can do and they see video games with foul language where they are talking to each other in profane ways. It all adds up to kids thinking, 'I can do it too; it is cool when they do it, so I will too'.

Sharisa T. Robertson:

How does bullying negatively impact the victim and the bully? Can this also impact them in their adulthood?

Juanita Tookes:

I believe that the answer is within the questions because bullying affects both parties. I know that the girls that bullied me, when we got older, I reconnected with, of course, through Facebook. I accepted her friendship, but I was shocked by her reaching out to me, considering what she had done to me. She liked a lot of my posts, had a lot of positive things to say about me, and even sent me encouraging messages.

It made me laugh because I was thinking, were you not in the same class as me, and do you not remember anything that had happened? I was amazed by all of this positivity because when I initially met her she was very negative. A lot of people don't care to think about how they were in school. Their perspective is that you just need to get over it. 'This happened when we were kids, so whatever.'

I think it is always important to think about how you treat people because you treat people how you want to be treated. A lot of times people are experiencing things in their adulthood because of how they were treated when they were younger. So as far as the aggressor, some individuals feel guilty and remorseful. For some bullies it increases awareness because sometimes things will come back to get you through the experiences of your children.

When someone has a child, they have a high sensitivity and high awareness because they know what they were like when they were in school. So they try to teach lessons from what they use to do, and how it was wrong, and for their child to not to do that to others or hang around those that are aggressive.

Some bullies can have a negative self-reflection of themselves, especially if they never see the person again that they bullied; it may sit with them and they may become bothered by it. This is for those who choose to do self-monitoring. There are some that again believe that that was back then; 'I was young, get over it....I did'. So not everybody looks at themselves in that state and says, 'I should have made different choices back then'. So some do and some don't. It is easier for the aggressor to not be bothered by it because they were not the ones that experienced the bullying.

On the other hand, the one being bullied of course, has a more obvious negative outcome as far as not being able to interact with people properly growing up, being afraid in social situations, and negative interactions with people in the future.

For both parties though, this is one of the main features in psychology and one of the main things that I look at and believe. What one does as a child, if they are having trouble or experiencing trauma, or if something bad happens to you, even if it is just one isolated incident; if the issue is not resolved and processed properly, it will follow you all the way up to adulthood, and you will experience problems. In adulthood, because the childhood issues hasn't been resolved, when I work with these individuals, when I look at them, I don't see, let's say a thirty-eight-year-old person, I see a ten-year-old child. This describes most of my clients, no matter the physical age; I see them as their inner child due to their unresolved childhood issues. Most of the time, any problems being faced in the present, can be tied back to something in their past as a child. We have so many children in grown people bodies.

I can say the same has happened with me, due to what I experienced as a child affected me as an adult. That is why it is so important that as parents when you see something, even if it is just an inkling that something is wrong with your child, whether through behavior, how they talk, etc. They need help by you to process that and have explained to them that the negativity from their behavior can affect them, and assure them that there is help.

But more importantly, that if this isn't solved now, these issues can manifest and spread like cancer, and then as time goes on it can be harder to deal with and get rid of. Because when we get to an adult age our mindsets, beliefs, and position is a little more concrete. At a young age, they are just like clay that can be molded, shaped, but as we get older that mold starts to solidify and is harder to try and shape and mold.

In general, I do believe that there can and will be negative effects for the aggressor and the person being bullied, and can have devastating effects as far as their adult interactions and experiences go.

Sharisa T. Robertson:

This may be a farfetched question, but is there something positive that can come from being bullied (life lessons, knowing how to handle difficult people, how to prepare for the real world, etc.)?

Juanita Tookes:

Yes, and that is not a crazy question. Those who choose to not let bullying control them for the rest of their lives that is exactly what they have learned. The biggest life lesson that they can learn is that this is not the only person that they are going to meet like this. Even in the workplace, trust me; you meet some of the same types of people.

When I started working at my first real office job while getting my bachelors, I was there for six years; my last supervisor was a bully. When I say bully, I mean it. I would go in the bathroom and cry. She was very mean and belittled me constantly. She was very callous, cold, and inconsiderate. She jerked me around a lot and completely abused her power. The sight of her would sometimes provoke severe anxiety, headaches, stress, and fatigue within me. It was bad. So bullying is not just limited to the age range of underage children. Adults suffer bullying too it is just in a different domain, in this case occupational bullying.

In encountering bullying early on it doesn't come across as much of a shock when you get older and come into contact with adult bullies, and if so it would be because you don't expect an adult to act like a child. When you are younger, bullying isn't accepted but it is expected. Children are still trying to figure out who they are. There are a lot that they don't know; they are naïve, and trying to find their way. Some adults are carrying these same traits into their adulthood, and they project it on to others. So a lot of adults are still naïve, still trying to learn who they are, still trying to find their way, but it isn't acceptable and is looked down upon because of the expected maturity that should come with age.

Although very unfortunate, I do think that you can learn very valuable lessons from being bullied, including the child learning who they are and their true strength. These lessons can take you through elementary school, high school, the workplace and other areas in life. You will meet people that you don't click with, people who are mean, people who don't treat you right, but in spite of that you have to look over and above that at the bigger goal.

Both parties can learn, but the most important thing is to remember the lessons. If we try to leave things in the past without learning from them then when we encounter them again it throws us off and we are shocked. Parents have a duty to keep in the forefront of their child's mind that everyone isn't as you think.

That is why parenting is so important. Parents can reinforce the lessons so when their child gets older they can say my mother/father told me about this. But if a parent isn't instilling these lessons and pushing certain types of values now, an older child or adult may not be prepared and feel like the rug has been pulled out from under them.

Sharisa T. Robertson:

So in going deeper into parenting, how can a parent help their child if they are being bullied or if they are a bully?

Juanita Tookes:

It is so hard for parents. The main thing that I think prevents children from speaking up is fear that the situation may get worse. Sometimes as parents we can't worry about it getting worse if they, or we, speak up about the bullying because it continue to get worse, even if no one says anything about it. If no one says anything, it will keep happening and escalate as times goes on. If they do say something, something may happen because they are now perceived as a tattle-tell or snitch. But if something is going to happen anyway, then you may as well do it the right way and speak out about it. As parents, you cannot always cater to the wishes of your children because they think it will be better a certain way.

However, there are certain ways that things can be done. It is best if all of the parents meet with the principal including all kids involved. This is so everyone is equally represented so when things are stated everyone hears it at the same time. This will allow for addressing of questions, gaining clarity, taking ownership, and planning the next steps that need to be taken, and everyone is on one accord knowing what the result is or could be.

Now in theory this sounds helpful but it is only effective if all of the parents show up. I find that when the parents show up it is then that you will see where the behavior stems from. Lots of time parents will deny, make excuses, become very defensive, and not take ownership for the behavior of their child. They portray the person that has been bullied as if they were, or did, something wrong, were deserving of the treatment, or downplay their child's behavior as if it is no big deal. We have to wonder when parents behave like this, what kind of message is being sent to the child.

Parental behavior is very important in shaping and molding the behavior of that child. Children will continue to do what you let them do, and they will continue to do what they see you, the parent, do. So if the parent is going off on the principal and the other parent, why do they think that their child is being a bully and displaying aggressive behavior? If a parent can become aggressive among a room full of strangers, it can only be imagined what is taking place outside of school among people they are familiar with, especially in the company of their child.

There is also the reality that some parents may not even come to the meeting to try and resolve the issue and get a full understanding and report of what is occurring. They, too, may be dealing with some issues. Maybe the parent feels guilty about coming to the meeting because they know that their absence in their child's life, whether physically or emotionally, can be the reason why the child is bullying as a way of lashing out.

Many parents are absent in the emotional aspect, but may be physically present. That is a form of neglect which is still in my opinion a form of abuse, regardless of what the reason behind it is. Sometimes parents have limited options and choices but some parents are just there, but not "there." They are in the home, see their child daily, but there is no emotional connection, they are emotionally unavailable. They are not aware of what is going on with their child from the biggest to the smallest details. They are not active, nor are they participating in the lives of their child, but in everything they do or don't do, it is still contributing something (good or bad) to that child. This can lead to very detrimental results for that child if the parent is not present in their home life and school life.

I deal with children every day whose parents are resistant and it is at the sacrifice of their child's well-being, psychologically and emotionally. It all goes back to the root of the parents failing to deal with their issues, so they are unable or unwilling, to deal with the issues of their children. So many children are dealing with the issues of their parents. They are mimicking the issues of their parents. But then the parents are signing the child up for therapy when in essence it isn't the child, it is the parent who needs help! The child is acting out because the parent is acting out, and the parent doesn't know what to do with them because they don't know what to do with their selves.

The issues can only be resolved by those who seek a resolution regardless of what side of the issue they are on. But ultimately, once the parent gets their self together, all of the problems they have seen within their child will begin to go away or severely diminish.

Parents have to step out of their pride and admit that they have a problem and want to seek help, so they can help their child. Every parenting problem/issue) will be different, but a problem is a problem regardless of what it is, especially compared to others; it is about how it affects you and the child as well. But the blame has to stop being placed solely on the child, saying that they are the problem.

Sharisa T. Robertson:

Are teachers/principals missing the signs of bullying? Are schools equipped to handle the magnitude in which bullying has become?

Juanita Tookes:

I work with a lot of schools. There is something that off puts me with the schools. I understand that teachers can have 35-40 students, but if a child is being bullied then something needs to happen. There is a girl who I see whose school I had to visit several times in the school year because she was getting bullied. Then at the same time she was pinpointed because she had a mental diagnosis, and so they thought it was just her and her behavioral issues, because she is a special needs child. She told me that she had been getting bullied for quite some time and when she told her teacher, nothing was done about it. The bullying continued, and a note was sent home. I am not a fan of notes being sent home because they can get lost or thrown away. Long story short, the girl was suspended for inappropriate behavior.

As a psychologist, I came in to examine the situation and see what was going on. In my findings, I saw that the school was just looking at the surface issue of the victim because of her special needs and behaviors associated with that. I had to show them that the behaviors had been showing because she was dealing with ongoing bullying for months, and it was not being handled at all. Her father tried calling the school, and they gave him the run around. When I called, they tried to give me the run around too, but I don't play that when it comes to kids and bullying. I have no problem showing my face until we get answers.

I was given a pamphlet about the policy having zero tolerance on bullying and paperwork. All of that is great and needed, but it has to be adhered to and put into place. I believe a lot of times schools are not equipped to handle the bullying beyond the black and white print policy. A policy is only good when it is being implemented.

Some schools are not equipped to handle bullying or they are not used to doing any hands on work in relation to bullying. When I say hands on, I am referring to the school assembly, group meetings, utilizing and having a school counselor or psychologist, and them becoming someone that can be trusted and easy to talk to.

Also, there needs to be continual maintenance, as in a poll or survey conducted to get anonymous feedback on what the level of bullying is going on in real life within the school. The poll/survey can ask questions like, 'are you experiencing any bullying' within certain duration of time. Just so that the school can see the actual results of what is taking place. Questions can ask if anybody has witnessed bullying and even ask does the child believe that they are a bully or have bullying tendencies'. So much more can be asked and addressed, and I believe the results of that can be astounding and informative for the school, about what may not be reported or missed. Then they can figure out an action plan on how to tend to the issue and reinforce their policy along with developing hands on solutions.

In the same token, I know that schools are trying to do the best that they can, considering the capacity that they are operating with and in. They have many students within their schools to deal with. They also get false reporting of bullying and incidents that can take up their time and resources. I know the schools that I have worked with are so overwhelmed with the work of monitoring, teaching all of the children at once, and the behind the scenes things we don't see, for them to function every day. So bullying is one of those things that, unfortunately, slip through the cracks or get placed on the bottom of the list as far as what to address; especially when it isn't as obvious at times to prove and see.

Sharisa T. Robertson:

We discussed that children are more aggressive compared to back in the day, but are children more sensitive these days, in regards to being bullied and their response or lack of response of not sticking up for themselves? Also taking into consideration the number of children who are committing suicide or hurting themselves (cutting, drugs, alcohol, etc.) due to being bullied.

Juanita Tookes:

I wouldn't say that they are more sensitive. I just think that after so much time and endurance of bullying they give up. Their level of motivation and ability to push through is severely decreased. After going through the same situation so many times and nothing has changed, what is to stop you from becoming frustrated and losing hope? They may begin to ask, 'what is the point of living here if this is what my life is going to be?'

Feeling like they have nobody to depend on, and even if they too begin to act out, now they are getting in trouble for what is really a cry for help and attention. One begins to get tired of everything. Tired of being ignored, ran over, of going to the principal and teachers and getting no results, of being told by a parent just to go to school and deal with it. Kids get tired of not having anywhere to go in a maze of bullying, where they are constantly hitting against brick walls with no open door anywhere.

Sensitivity is something that is developed in a certain spot after it has been hit so much. Now that spot is sore and every time it is touched, that is when the child either cries, walks away, gives up, hurt themselves, bottles things in, or act out.

Sharisa T. Robertson:

So in saying that, how do we tell a child to keep fighting, to not give up, to take a stand, and/or handle being bullied? I do realize that there may not be an exact right answer to this.

Juanita Tookes:

Yes, you are right. There isn't an exact right answer. All of the things that were mentioned, like having the meetings, reporting it when it happens, parents getting involved, instilling within your child lessons and confidence, understanding the context of their psychological and emotional well-being ….sometimes at the end of the day none of it works and what could be for a number of reasons that will be dependent upon each individual base based on who is involved, the duration of everything taking place, the action steps being taken, and being consistent in it all. If everything has been done, including going to higher officials, getting support, maybe even changing schools, and bullying seems to starts at a new school, or maybe it is in the neighborhood and you can't move, parents have to be there for their child.

In these cases, as the bullying is happening and when it still seems to persist, as a child is going through it, I heavily suggest that the parent needs to be in full support of their child during these times and be the source of emotional support. Let them know that they can talk to you, sympathize with what they are going through, protect them as much as you can, fight for them, see them through it, and make a lesson out of it about dealing with difficult people throughout our lives, remind and assure them of who they are and their worth, and help build their confidence. But just love them and be there for them.

Sharisa T. Robertson:

What are your thoughts on taking legal matters, like pressing charges against the other child? Is that going too far or when should that be taken into consideration?

Juanita Tookes:

The legal aspect in any matter should be the last resort. After you have done all you can do to resolve the situation civically and it is still continuing, then you have the right to take legal action. You should consult for legal advice and have documentation.

You don't want to result to legal actions because not only is it costly (depending on what kind of actions you are taking) but they may not want to actually press charges against another child. But if it persists, taking legal action may, and is, the strongest message you can send out there that you are not playing around, and you will not stand for this. But again, this is an extreme measure and should be a last resort, and hopefully a resort you want have to go to.

Sharisa T. Robertson:

In regards to the bully, bullies are instantly labeled. How do we help them too, and see them as a victim outside of just giving them a consequence (suspension, kicked out of school, legal action) and provide a solution for them as well so hardships don't continue in their lives?

Juanita Tookes:

That is a very good point you bring up because even though this is mostly about the child being bullied, it is also about the "bully" as well. We have to not be so quick to slap a label on a child while neglecting the fact that they too are suffering in some way.

There have been cases where legally a parent has taken charges against the school, and has talked to a professional saying that they don't want to take action against a child but can counseling, community service, mentoring, or something that will help them to learn and grow from this experience, while still holding them accountable for their actions, be enforced? A consequence is needed, but isn't enough because after suspension, after getting kicked out of school, after going to juvenile detention, once it is over, they are back to doing the same thing and maybe even worse now than before.

I think forcing them to work through their problems is better than just slap sticking a label and a suspension on them. Maybe even having them have family counseling as well, because sometimes charges can be put on the parent/guardian and not the child. But there isn't a lesson being learned from being suspended all the time or going to juvy, and if there is a lesson, is it a positive one or is it a negative one from a negative experience?

I work in the juvenile system as well, so I see the kids in there who come in with a chip on their shoulder and now they feel like they have to prove something. When they leave they still feel like they have something to prove, but under all of that, they are still hurt little kids, scared even. Their problems still have not been dealt with. They are still dealing with whatever is going on in their lives that is the root cause of what we see and how they act.

So, just as you said, we had to stop with the labels and not give up on a child because that child will find someone else to lash out at. If you seek legal help, be willing to ask how you can help the other child because isn't always about getting money or pressing charges; we can be advocates for other kids, even those that may be the ones hurting ours. It takes a lot to do it, but it can be done, or at least we have to try.

Sharisa T. Robertson:

How would you advise a bully to change if they wanted to change and redeem themselves? Can a bully redeem themselves after all they have done?

Juanita Tookes:

The answer is right there.....changing your behavior. If a bully wants to redeem themselves and doesn't want that label anymore, they will have to stop acting like that label. A conscious choice would have to be made, and the bully will have to decide and declare that they will not continue to do what they have been doing, and that they will do things differently.

Of course, this can apply to anything in life, whether that's wanting to turn away from drugs, being a recovering alcoholic, or stopping being physically abusive. It isn't an easy thing to do, but it is necessary if you want different results in your life, you have to make the decision to do and act differently. If a bully doesn't want to be perceived as a bully, then they have to show themselves, and act, in another light.

Even the Bible says if you want to make friends then you have to show yourself friendly (Proverbs 18:24). Maybe you (the bully) haven't communicated that in the best way to your social group. So instead of using intimidation, power, and control to make friends, use friendlier tactics instead. You have to begin to gain the trust of others, especially those who knew you as a bully; but things like simply introducing yourself, enrolling in an after school program to start building social relationships, and counseling can aid in developing social skills. Even if you don't know how to make things different, you will look for different resources to try to help you make them different.

Sharisa T. Robertson:

How do we stop bullying, or is bullying going to always be around?

Juanita Tookes:

When I think about that question, I think about racism. Will racism always exist? Can we stop it? The answer is yes and no. We all may have the hope that racism will cease, but based on past events and patterns and what has happened historically, racism has never left. In fact, it may be even worse; it is just expressed differently in many ways. But can we stop it? We can try.

There is no absolute when it comes to things like this because it all involves a multitude of different dispositions and perceptions. The only one we can change is ourselves.

It starts with each of us. We can't change the actions, behaviors, or cognition of another. We can hope to influence and/or inspire them by our change, but it is ultimately each person's decision. But hopefully that change can become a domino effect to stop it where we can stop it. The same with bullying because bullying has a history as well.

This isn't to say we shouldn't try, because we should always try to stop, prevent, or lessen anything that is not right in our society, especially when it is something as hurtful and impactful as this. There are so many organizations and resources to assist us in reaching a multitude of people.

So we can and should try to influence the behavior of the majority to change how they think and act, but the thing with behavior is that it is an individual choice.

I even tell my clients that it is not my job to get you to do what I think is best; it is about helping you think about what it is you should do. This is regardless if I am seeing an adult for substance abuse, alcohol, or something else. The purpose is to think before you drink, think before you bully, think before you take drugs, think before you act, and think about the consequences if you do it and continue doing it, think about making a different choice than what you are used to, think about what would be a different, but better outcome, think about how to achieve that.

If we can plant a seed about getting people to truly think about their actions before they actually act, there will be a higher probability of changing the behavior versus trying to hit them over the head with lectures and books, telling them what they should or shouldn't be doing. People are more likely to rebel when they are being made to do something, and if they are being made to do something then that means they didn't want to do it to begin with. But with planting the seeds with suggestions, you get their wheels turning, and you are more likely to produce some change, versus you coming down on them.

I believe this applies to bullying as well, and not just the bully, but the person being bullied, and the parents as well. Bullying has been around for a long time, and although I don't want to put an absolute on it and say yes, we can stop it, I will say we can certainly try to stop it. We should, must try to stop it. These kids' future and livelihoods depend on us trying, and trying our best, and trying with our all.

Juanita Tookes MA, TLLP
(Masters in arts, temporary limited license psychologist)

About the Contributor

Juanita Tookes, age 29, was born and raised in Detroit MI, and has worked diligently to overcome obstacles placed in her way. At the age of ten she knew that she wanted to grow up and become a doctor. At age seventeen she knew more specifically that she wanted to be a psychologist, in order to help the bond between marriages and families become stronger so that they could stay together. The importance of education was not stressed in her household however the world around her showed her the significance of receiving higher learning. Juanita successfully completed high school in 2003 and went on to earn her bachelor's degree in psychology in 2008 from Wayne State University. After two years of rest from college life, Juanita applied and was accepted into the master's program at Wayne State in 2010. Working a full-time job and being a full-time student was very difficult but she worked hard and continued to press forward, and in May of 2013 she received her master's degree in counseling psychology. Today Juanita is a successful master's level psychologist working with individuals, couples, families, and persons with developmental disabilities. Juanita is gaining the knowledge and experience to ultimately help her attain her doctorate degree.

Afterword

In order to combat the bullying that has become so much more rampant, scathing and downright dangerous in recent years, the first thing we, as protectors of children, need to focus on is SELF-LOVE. Not only to help children be strong enough to combat bullying, but also as a means of preventing bullying altogether.

As a social worker and licensed therapist, who has worked in the field for nearly a decade, I cannot express how often the root to a conflict has been a lack of self-love. When a child bullies, we can almost always guarantee that there is a lack of self-esteem present. If they don't value themselves or see themselves as the fearfully and wonderfully made creations of God that they are, one of the most prominent ways this is manifested, is through the devaluing of others, in an attempt to gain value themselves.

While we cannot make a child love themselves, we can teach them how, through a number of ways. One of the most important being, modeling. When the children in your life see you, do they see a person that loves and values themselves?

Do they see a person who can handle conflict in a calm, peaceful manner? Do they see a person who takes pride in their appearance, job, positive interactions with others, etc.? Do they see a person who can take correction with grace? Or do they see someone who hides behind a facade of loud talk, revealing clothing, gossip or whatever other walls we put up to shield ourselves from the glares of the outside world.

The days of "do as I say, not as I do" are over. Just, in the same way, that our girls learn how to tie their shoes, put on makeup, or cook, they also get their first ideas of self-concept from observing the behavior of those around them.

Another way we can teach the concept of self-love is to, as the author mentioned at the beginning of this book, affirm our young girls. Young girls who feel affirmed don't feel the need to abuse others in an unhealthy effort to give themselves value. They are too busy focusing on the positive, to even give the mental space to negative interactions with others. Girls who have been affirmed in the home or family are less likely to be as negatively affected by attempts from bullying, as they already have a built in defense to combat the negativity that was leveled toward them.

Finally, reinforcement and accountability. As we know that all youth will experience bullying at some point in their life, these two are vitally important. When you suspect that your child has been bullied, it is important to reinforce that child's positive self-talk and coping skills to assist them in combating the problem. Also reinforcing the fact that you are there to take action on their behalf, as often children believe they have to go at this alone.

Hold your child accountable. If you ever observe even the slightest hint of bully behavior in your child, address it immediately. They may be unaware that their behavior is unhealthy. Educate them and let them know that this behavior is unacceptable.

Bullying is the fruit on a large tree. We cannot just cut the fruit from the tree; we have to dig it up from the roots. It can be done, but it takes effort, resilience, and self-awareness. Once we, as adults, become healthy, we can pass these behaviors down to our children.

Rhea J. Cooper, LMSW

Resources

Facts and Statistics

- ➢ A girl is bullied every seven minutes
- ➢ 15% of girls who are bullied tell someone
- ➢ Almost 1/3 of girls are directly involved in bullying, either by being bullied, or by being a bully
- ➢ 43% of girls fear harassment in the bathroom
- ➢ When girl bullying occurs, 85% of the time there is no interventions, 11% of peer intervention, 4% teacher intervention
- ➢ Each day 160,000 students miss school due to bullying
- ➢ 1 in 7 students (children/youth) from kindergarten to 12th grade have been bullied
- ➢ Studies show that, up until the age of 4, both boys and girls show aggression in the same way, by grabbing toys from other kids or even pushing. But, at the age of four, most girls have started to develop ways to manipulate other kids and to exclude others. (Sub-adolescent Queen Bees) By the time they reach five, they are really good at gossiping, telling lies and secrets to exclude some of their peers. So even before kindergarten girls know how to perform relational aggression. Relational aggression is often used to describe the type of bullying that females specialize in. Instead of bullying defenseless kids that they don't know, females bully those that are closest to them. Female bullying is used to create a social hierarchy of the privileged and the oppressed. In many ways, this is psychological warfare at its finest. It is a form of both psychological and emotional abuse that uses relationships as a way to inflict injury to other peers.
- ➢ Sometimes referred to as emotional bullying, or the mean girl phenomenon, relational aggression involves social manipulation, such as excluding others from the group, spreading rumors, breaking confidences, and getting others to dislike another person.
- ➢ In general, girls tend to be more relationally aggressive than boys, especially during the tween and teen years. It is especially intense among girls in fifth grade through eighth grade.
- ➢ While the tactics used in relational aggression vary from person to person, there are some common behaviors in this type of bullying. These include:
  - ○ Talking badly about others
  - ○ Spreading rumors or participating in gossip
  - ○ Breaking confidences or sharing secrets
  - ○ Building alliances among social circles
  - ○ Backstabbing one another
  - ○ Using code names to talk about others
  - ○ Making fun of others for who they are, the way they dress or how they look
  - ○ Excluding and ostracizing others
  - ○ Leaving hurtful or mean messages on cell phones, on desks or in lockers

- o Huddling together and whispering about others
- o Intimidating others with stares or certain looks
- o Using hostile body language such as smirks and eye-rolling
- o Encouraging others to ignore or exclude certain people
- o Engaging in cyber bullying
- o Source: http://bullying.about.com/od/Basics/a/What-Is-Relational-Aggression-And-Why-Do-Kids-Engage-In-It.htm

➤ Girls bully by using emotional violence. They do things that make others feel alienated and alone. Some of the tactics used by girls who bully include:
- o Anonymous prank phone calls or harassing emails from dummy accounts
- o Playing jokes or tricks designed to embarrass and humiliate
- o Deliberate exclusion of other kids for no real reason
- o Whispering in front of other kids with the intent to make them feel left out?
- o Name calling, rumor spreading and other malicious verbal interactions
- o Being friends one week and then turning against a peer the next week with no incident or reason for the alienation
- o Encouraging other kids to ignore or pick on a specific child
- o Inciting others to act out aggressively or violently

➤ Why a young woman who is bullied may not ask for help:
- o She may be afraid to stand up for herself or voice her opinions.
- o She is too afraid to get help from anyone, especially adults.
- o She may not have her friends around and feels unable to defend herself.
- o She is seen as different from everyone else because of her age, weight, clothing, family, money, race, ethnicity, and religion. She may also have different ideas and hobbies that others think are weird.
- o (I would add that she may not like to have confrontations, she may think sticking up for herself will make things worse, she may just hope she will be left alone, she may feel like if she says something it will draw more attention from more people, she may not understand why she is even being bullied, she may be embarrassed.)
- o Source: http://girlshealth.gov/bullying/whybullied/

➤ Many young women who are bullied do not try to stop the bullies. This may be because they do not know many other teen girls are also bullied each year. Some teens are so afraid of losing their friends that they go along with what others say and do, even if it is mean and hurts themselves or other people. So why do certain people get bullied? Why are they bullied more than others? Typically, bullies often pick on:
- o People they are jealous of
- o Girls who will not fight back
- o People who seem "different" from themselves or their friends
- o Teens who may be "richer" or "poorer" than the bully
- o Girls who hit puberty earlier or later than others in the class

- o   People with a disability
- o   Source: http://girlshealth.gov/bullying/whybullied/
- ➢   In Girls, Bullying Behaviors and Peer Relationships: The Double-Edged Sword of Exclusion and Rejection, Barbara Leckie explains how bullying by girls manifests itself and how it is handled by adults. Leckie went over numerous studies dating back as far as 1980, and identified the many different ways that girls bully. She also found that adults were slower to react to the bullying tactics used by girls. If there is violence or physically acting out of any sort adults are quick to intervene and when necessary will punish offenders, but when the bullying takes on a less obvious form even adults don't seem to know what to do. When girls bully it often goes unaddressed. Since adults don't always label the tactics used by girls as bullying kids who fall, victim don't know where to turn for help.

  The mindset still exists that not all kids can be friends and the social structure of the school system encourages the formation of groups and reinforces the idea of social hierarchies. This makes many adults slow to recognize things like exclusion and alienation as something sinister. These behaviors are often dismissed as an unfortunate part of the normal formation of peer groups.

  While it is normal for girls and boys to form social groups and close bonds with certain people at the exclusion of others, it becomes bullying when those groups make power plays over other groups or individuals. Having friends is one thing: having friends who work to make others feel that they are not good enough to be included is another. Playing the popularity game in a way that causes fear or inadequacy in others is a form of bullying, and it is a common tactic used by girls.

- ➢   The typical girl who bullies is popular, well-liked by adults, does well in school, and can even be friends with the girls she bullies. She doesn't get into fist fights, although some girls who bully do. Instead, she spreads rumors, gossips..., excludes others, shares secrets, and teases girls about their hair, weight, intelligence, and athletic ability. She usually bullies in a group and others join in or pressure her to bully.

  http://www.ncpc.org/topics/bullying/girls-and-bullying

- ➢   When most people picture a "typical" bully, they imagine a boy who is bigger or older than his classmates, who doesn't do well in school, who fights, and who likes it when others are scared of him. Girls usually face a different type of bully, one who may not look as scary from the outside, but who can cause just as much harm.
- ➢   What's She Like:
  - o   The typical girl who bullies is popular, well-liked by adults, does well in school, and can even be friends with the girls she bullies. She doesn't get into fist fights, although some girls who bully do. Instead, she spreads rumors, gossips, excludes others, shares secrets, and teases girls about their hair, weight, intelligence, and athletic ability. She usually bullies in a group and others join in or pressure her to bully.
- ➢   The Effects:

- This kind of bullying can have just as serious consequences as physical bullying. It can cause a drop in grades, low self-esteem, anxiety, depression, drug use, and poor eating habits in girls who are bullied. This kind of bullying is harder to see. Most of the time adults don't realize when girls are being bullied in this way.
- Source: http://www.ncpc.org/topics/bullying/girls-and-bullying

➤ Study shows bullying can cause physical illnesses in kids
- Headaches
- Backaches
- Problems sleeping
- Bedwetting
- Stomachaches
- Poor eating habits
- Trouble eating
- Nausea
- Diarrhea
- Shoulder pain
- Tense muscles
- Trouble breathing
- Source:http://www.metroparent.com/Blogs/Views-on-the-News/September-2013/Bullying-Can-Cause-Physical-Illness-in-Kids-Study-Says/

➤ Examples of types of bullying (but not limited to what is mentioned and can be a combination of what is listed):
- Cyber- Takes place using electronic technology
  - Sending mean text messages, emails, social media posts/private messages
  - Spreading rumors via e-mail, text, social media sites
  - Sharing embarrassing pictures or videos via e-mail, text, social media
  - Hacking into someone's account and acting like them by sending false messages or e-mail meant to ruin their reputation or hacking into their account to retrieve info to use to embarrass/gossip
- Cyber fighting- Intentionally starting arguments, threats, picking on someone online
- Cyber stalking- following someone online to different groups, social media sites, harassing them
- Cyber tricking- Tricking someone to reveal something personal to you via online and using that information against them
- Cyber exclusion- Leaving someone out of an online group purposely with a negative intent
- Verbal- Saying or writing mean things
  - Teasing

- Name calling
- Taunting
- Inappropriate sexual comments
- Threatening to cause harm
  - o Physical- hurting somebody's body or possessions
    - Hitting, kicking, pinching
    - Spitting
    - Tripping, pushing, pulling someone's hair
    - Taking or breaking someone's thing
    - Making rude hand gestures
  - o Social- hurting someone's reputation or relationships
    - Leaving someone out on purpose
    - Telling other children not to be friends with someone
    - Spreading rumors
    - Embarrassing somebody in public
  - o Source: via Internet info graphics
  - o Bullying can also take place in the form of hazing and blackmail
- ➤ Cyber bullying facts
  - o 32% of online teens say they have been targets of a range of annoying or potentially menacing online activities. 15% of teens overall say someone has forwarded or posted a private message they've written. 13% say someone has spread a rumor about them online, 13% say someone has sent them a threatening or aggressive message, and 6% say someone has posted embarrassing pictures of them online.
  - o 38% of online girls report being bullied compared with 26% of online boys. In particular, 41% of older girls (15-17) report being bullied— more than any other age or gender group.
  - o 39% of social network users have been cyber bullied in some way, compared with 22% of online teens who do not use social networks.
  - o 20% of teens (12-17) say, "People are mostly unkind" on online social networks. Younger teenage girls (12-13) are considerably more likely to say this. One in three (33%) younger teen girls who use social media say that people their age are "mostly unkind" to one another on social network sites.
  - o 15% of teens on social networks have experienced someone being mean or cruel to them on a social networking site. There are no statistically significant differences by age, gender, race, socioeconomic status, or any other demographic characteristic.
  - o 13% of teens who use social media (12-17) say they have had an experience on a social network that made them feel nervous about going to school the next day. This is more common among younger teens (20%) than older teens (11%).

- 88% of social media-using teens say they have seen someone be mean or cruel to another person on a social network site. 12% of these say they witness this kind of behavior "frequently."
- When teens see others being mean or cruel on social networks, frequently 55% see other people just ignoring what is going on, 27% see others defending the victim, 20% see others telling the offender to stop, and 19% see others join in on the harassment.
- 36% of teens who have witnessed others being cruel on social networks have looked to someone for advice about what to do.
- 67% of all teens say bullying and harassment happens more offline than online.
- 1 in 6 parents knows their child has been bullied over social media. In over half of these cases, their child was a repeat victim. Over half of parents whose children have social media accounts are concerned about cyber bullying and more than three-quarters of parents have discussed the issue of online bullying with their children.
- 11% of middle school students were victims of cyber bullying in the past two months. Girls are more likely than boys to be victims or bully/victims.
- "Hyper-networking" teens (those who spend more than three hours per school day on online social networks) are 110% more likely to be a victim of cyber bullying, compared to those who don't spend as much time on social networks.
- Source:http://www.covenanteyes.com/2012/01/17/bullying-statistics-fast-facts-about-cyberbullying/
- Only 7% of U.S. parents are worried about cyber bullying, yet 33% of teenagers have been victims of cyber bullying
- 1 million children were harassed, threatened or subjected to other forms of cyber bullying on FACEBOOK during the past year.

- Bullying and Violence
  - 86% of students said, "Other kids picking on them, making fun of them or bullying them" causes teenagers to turn to lethal violence in schools.
  - 87% of students said shootings are motivated by a desire to "get back at those who have hurt them."
  - 61% of students said students shoot others because they have been victims of physical abuse at home.
  - 54% of students said witnessing physical abuse at home can lead to violence in school.
  - 282,000 students are physically attacked in secondary schools each month.
  - Those in the lower grades reported being in twice as many fights as those in the higher grades. However, there is a lower rate of serious violent crimes in the elementary level than in the middle or high schools.

- 90% of 4th through 8th graders report being victims of bullying.
- Bullying statistics say revenge is the strongest motivation for school shootings.
- Harassment and bullying have been linked to 75% of school-shooting incidents.
- Among students, homicide perpetrators were more than twice as likely as homicide victims to have been bullied by peers.
- Source: http://www.nveee.org/statistics/

➤ A new review of studies from 13 countries found signs of an apparent connection between bullying, being bullied, and suicide. (Yale School of Medicine)

➤ Bullycide is a term used to describe suicide as the result of bullying

➤ Girls can also bully boys, and this type of bullying goes unnoticed or ignored because the girl is an aggressor to a boy who is expected to just 'toughen up' and deal with it

➤ Boys can also bully girls. It can be physical or using or in a threatening manner that uses his strength as a male, or his power/status, or connection to girls (sister/friend) that may be considered tough as leverage. It can sometimes be in the form of sexual bullying which is the same or similar to sexual harassment that is unwanted and used to control, embarrassment, or hurt the girl

➤ Bullying may be more common amongst the same gender but bullying amongst opposite gender is overlooked and ignored

➤ Biracial and multiracial youth are more likely to be victimized than youth who identify with a single race.

➤ Kids who are obese, gay, or have disabilities are up to 63% more likely to be bullied than other children.

➤ Academically gifted students, especially those with high verbal aptitude, are often bullied and are more likely than less gifted students to suffer emotionally

➤ Bullies are more likely to engage in vandalism, shoplifting, truancy, and substance abuse than students who do not bully during early childhood. There is also a direct correlation between substance abuse and gun violence and bullying behavior

➤ It is a myth that bullying will most likely go away when it is ignored. Ignoring bullies reinforces to them that they can bully without consequence.

➤ It is likely that if someone was bullied in school, they will also be bullied in the workforce

➤ American schools harbor approximately 2.1 million bullies and 2.7 million of their victims. (Dan Olweus, National School Safety Center)

➤ Students see an estimated four out of every five bullying occurrences at school and join in about 3/4 of the time.

➤ According to bullying statistics, 1 out of every ten students who drop out of school does so because of repeated bullying.

➤ Some additional Websites to check out:
- www.stopbullying.gov
- www.stopbullyingnow.com

- o www.bullying.org
- o www.pacer.org/bullying
- o www.pacerteensagainstbullying.org
- o www.thebullyproject.com
- o https://bullyfree.com/free-resources/facts-about-bullying

There are tons of resources; please take the time to research to become more informed or to seek help and/or guidance in your local area or online.

Pledge for Youth and Adults

I will not bully others.

I will not tolerate being bullied.

I will help someone who is being bullied.

I will try and help the person who is a bully, if they are open to change and assistance.

I will use the resources and people around me to help me with any problems I may be having, or see others having, whether I am the bully, the bullied, the bystander, or an adult.

I will not suffer in silence or act out in violence or harm against myself or others.

I will not ignore bullying, especially if I am an authority figure.

I will not expect myself or someone else to just deal with bullying.

I will respect the differences in others.

I will act in integrity, good character, and sound judgment.

I will turn my pain into a higher purpose.

I will recognize that I am powerful, use it for the greater good, not ignore it, not abuse it, and not make anyone else feel powerless but to empower others and myself.

I will take a stand against bullying.

Parent's Technology Contract

- I know that the Internet is an important resource for my children and that being familiar with it is a necessary skill. It can also be a wonderful place to visit, but I know that I must do my part to help keep my kids safe online.
- I will get to know the services and websites my child uses.
- I will set reasonable rules and guidelines for computer use by my children, including how much time they may spend online; I will encourage them to participate in offline activities as well. We will discuss these rules and post them near the computer as a reminder.
- I will not overreact if my child tells me about something "bad" he or she finds or does on the Internet.
- If my child does something that I do not approve of online we will have a calm conversation about my expectations and the reasons for our Internet rules. I understand that just taking away the Internet will not solve the problem.
- If I see my child is bullied online/phone I will go to whatever lengths to protect my child and ensure their safety.
- I will try to get to know my child's online friends and contacts just as I try to get to know his or her offline friends.
- I will try to put the home computer in a family area rather than in my child's bedroom.
- I will report suspicious and illegal activity and sites to the proper authorities and learn how to report abuse when necessary.
- I will frequently check to see where my kids have visited on the Internet and I will talk to them if I see something I'm concerned about or that I think is inappropriate.
- I will talk to my children about their social networking profiles; what they can and cannot post, who they should allow as friends and how to behave appropriately in their online interactions.
- I will learn about parental controls for filtering and blocking inappropriate Internet material from my children.
- I will be involved. I will spend time with my child and be a positive part of my child's on line activities and relationships—just as I am offline.
- I will also set an example for my child online, offline, on and off the phone as to how to conduct yourself by using proper etiquette.
- If my child continues to break our Internet rules after we have discussed them I will impose penalties for their actions including (but may not be limited to) taking away his or her computer, cell phone or other devices until the behavior changes.

Agree to the above:

_____

Parent's Signature and Date

_____

Child's Signature and Date

Child's Technology Contract

- I understand that the Internet and having a cell phone/tablet/ etc is a privilege.
- I understand that mom and dad may access and look at my files at any time.
- I understand that I can use the computer /Internet/cell phones for approved purposes only.
- I will respect the privacy of others who use this computer. I will not open, move, or delete files that are not in my personal directory.
- I will not download anything, open attachments, or install programs without first asking open attachments, or install programs without first asking mom or dad.
- I will not download, share, watch, read, research via computer, tablet, phone anything illegal, crude, sexual, pornographic, or inappropriate in any manner
- I will tell my parents my usernames and passwords, but always keep them private from everyone else.

My screen names/user names/social media accounts are:

_____

My passwords are:

_____

My email address(es) are:

_____

- I will not share my personal information or my parents' or family's with anyone online. This includes: name, address, telephone number, age, school name, credit card numbers, family information, etc. I will not post this information to my profiles even if I think only my friends will see it.
- I will treat others the way I want to be treated online.
- I will be respectful and never pick fights or post mean or threatening words.
- I will not post anything rude, offensive or threatening, send or forward images or information that might embarrass, harass or hurt someone, take anyone's personal information and use it to damage his or her reputation in anyway.
- I will never write text, email, share anything that I would not want mom or dad to see, this includes but not limited to pictures, graphics, videos, emoticons, written words, etc.
- If I see or read things that I think are bad, inappropriate or mean I will show my parents right away.
- If I ever feel uncomfortable, scared about an experience online, I will not respond, save the evidence (post, picture, e-mail), tell my parent, guardian, or other trusted adult immediately.
- I will tell my parents if I receive pictures or links that I didn't ask for, or that contain inappropriate content, bad, hateful or mean language or anything I think might not be right.
- I will think before posting and not post any personal information or images that could put me at risk, embarrass me, or damage my future.
- If I am feeling down, upset, sad, suicidal, self harming, depress, confused, curious, etc instead of going to social media, groups, online friends, site, calling, texting people to vent, complain, or post, even bottling it within I will confide in my parents these feelings so that we can talk it out or in a trusted adult (counselor, teacher, family member, hotline, doctor).

- I understand that while social media is a great tool for communication, I will be conscious and aware of what I share online or via phone whether good or bad, some things are better left unsaid and social media is a public site whereas my business may not need to be public knowledge.
- I will not use profanity or otherwise offensive language.
- I will not lie about my age.
- I will tell my parents about the people I meet online, even if they don't ask. I won't answer emails, IMs, messages or friend requests from people I don't know and my parents haven't approved.
- I will not do anything a person online asks me to unless my parents say it's ok, especially things I know they wouldn't approve of.
- I will not call, write to, or meet someone in person who I've met online unless my parents say ok and come with me.
- I will talk with my parents or guardians about our rules for going online, including how long I can be online, what sites I can visit, and who I can communicate with while online.
- Daily time and usage for online and cell phone activity:
- _____
- I will help my parents learn more about the Internet and understand what I do and where I go online.
- I understandthat mom and dad are willing to help me and will not punish me as long as th ese rules are followed.
- I know that sometimes my parents will supervise where I go online or use software to restrict some websites but I understand that they are doing this because they want to protect me online.
- I know that if I break this contract or the Internet rules that my parents and I have discussed they can take away my access to the Internet including my computer and phone until my behavior changes.

Agree to the above:

_____
Child's Signature and Date

_____
Parent's Signature and Date

Thank you for reading our book.

If you enjoyed it, won't you please take a moment to leave me a review at your favorite retailer?

ALTMB authors and contributors appreciate you!

Visionary's Bio

Since beginning her own road to forgiveness after living more than half of her life in anger, which stems from having a troublesome relationship with her mother, Sharisa T. Robertson began to take notice of the hurt in others and how it hindered not only them, but also everyone and everything around them.

Sharisa uses her testimony and journey of overcoming emotional, mental, financial, and sometimes physical, abuse from her mother and the lessons she has learned from her childhood to her adulthood as a driving force that started off with her helping women heal from their past, and change the present, while working towards the future. But her business is now evolving off into helping men and children as well, and going from personal to professional to educational settings and backgrounds.

She has shared her testimony, mission and/or delivered a message on several blog talk radio shows and prayer lines. In doing so, she was offered to be a participant in a book collaboration, which was Sharisa's debut as an author in *Cheers To Your Success: Women on the Rise and Owning Their Destiny* by Visionary, Carol Sankar. Her chapter is entitled *Makeup of a Masterpiece*. This opportunity was one of the many things that inspired her to start and self publish her own book collaboration (the first installment of the series) *A Letter To My Mother: A Daughter's Perspective* for women who have or had been negatively impacted by their relationship with their mother, and are still carrying the burden of hurt, pain, anger, and resentment. Eleven women were a part of this powerful book project from Michigan, Maryland, New York, Texas, Kentucky, California, and North Carolina.

Sharisa is an Author, Forgiveness Facilitator, Publisher and Entrepreneur. Using her love for writing and sharing stories, she has started a media company. Sharisa is currently penning two books (fiction and nonfiction) both shedding additional light and perspective on the strained mother and daughter relationship. She is also bringing positive release, healing and forgiveness to the youth by releasing her second book collaboration, *A Letter To My Bully: Sticks, Stones, and Words Do Hurt.* The book project includes 7 youth girl authors from ages 9-14 and 5 female experts all from Michigan, Maryland, Delaware, Illinois, Georgia, West Virginia, New York, Virginia, Pennsylvania, and Texas. Through Lilies of the Field Media, LLC, Sharisa uses the platform of creative arts in the form of storytelling and being a voice that addresses the internal issues and struggles that plague many, and not just through books, but soon to be documentaries, plays and more.

Be on the lookout for many upcoming projects and ventures.

www.sharisarobertson.com
www.lotfmedia.com

Acknowledgments

I give supreme thanks to God for blessing me with this vision and mission. I do not take it lightly, and although I faltered throughout, I didn't give up, and when I wanted to, He always sent me reminders and encouraged me that this was needed, and to go on.

I have to send thanks and my love for always supporting me, Desman. I appreciate you always being in my corner. I thank my father and mother-in-law too, for all that they have done for me and because of that I was able to focus on this project.

To my children, I love you three to life and beyond with all of my heart. De'Shaia and Italia, I thank you for being the inspiration behind this. Although it came out of something bad, you immediately saw this book as a way to bring good. You both are very strong and courageous. Keep walking into what God has for you, no matter what anyone says. You are different, and you should be. Why be like anybody else when you can just be yourself? This is just the beginning.

To my authors, the girls who helped make this book possible, Arianna, Dallas, Justine, Chante, and Clara, I am so grateful for you girls! Thank you for allowing me to share a little of you with the world. Thank you for your boldness through this journey. You have encouraged me, please know that. There is so much strength in you girls, and I hope you see it and use it for the greater good. The seven of you are not victims of bullying, but VICTORS of bullying, and it is your voice that will be heard forever, not just for yourselves, but for others. Watch out world for these seven young ladies! Girl Power!!!

Thank you to my Facebook friends, the moms of these young ladies who entrusted me with providing a platform for their daughters. Samonia, Jacinta, Christina, Feona, Darriel you ladies, and your husbands are the best. I thank you for seeing this vision and wanting your daughters to be a part of such a movement. I know this was new for us all in such a way. I salute you for taking your child's life into your hands by seeing the value in them and this book. Blessings to you!!

To the dynamic ladies who co-authored and contributed to this book taking it to another level, I thank you so much!! Dr. Derschaun, Bonetta, Juanita, Sara, Anita, Rhea and Dr. Nicole you made this book even more than what I envisioned, not just a book for our girls, but for adults to get some help and answers about their girls. And even more so, you stand as women who are successful not just on the outside, but inside as well, and that serves as a good example that our girls need, so that they too can grow up and be like you ladies, but in their own right. From psychologists, counselors, entrepreneurs, authors, great parents, principals, giving back to their community, and so much more and the sky is the limit!

You are also an example that women can be great and work together and not against each other, and be in support of one another. Thank you for, being what this book on how to move forward. You all gave me something to think about in so many areas of my life and my children's lives, and I am sure the readers can attest to that as well.

I also give thanks and acknowledgement to many others who have in some way contributed to me and this book throughout this journey, Dr. Sandra Smith, Ashley Sauls, and Natasha Beautiful Thought Anée for your support and recommendations to the women who made this project complete. LaTara Bussey, Carol Sankar, Angela Wesley, Robin Scott for your ideas and support. Jolene and Destanie Johnson for your part in the project.

To my editor, I appreciate your eye, input, support and understanding of the vision and contribution to this project!!! I am happy to be connected to you. Thank you!

Thank you to my graphic designer who always does great work.

Thank you to recording artist, TAJ, and her momager Tegi for partnering with us and allowing us to use her song, "U Can't Bully Me," as our theme song, further creating a movement speaking out against bullying and creating awareness (available on iTunes).

Please know if your name wasn't mentioned but you have contributed in some way, it was not intentional. I thank you as well!!!!! As a matter of fact, Thank you

_____ (fill in your name here) ☺

Sharisa T. Robertson

****

I am thankful that God is there for me. I love my mom, and I am happy that you made this book. I thank my mom and dad for always being there for me. I love all of my family. I am happy that the girls in the book who were bullied spoke out against bullying. Thank you to everybody who made this a good book to help other people.

Italia Samere Ventour

****

This is dedicated to everyone who has ever been put down by someone else. Remember to stay strong because you can live through it, you can survive it and you can overcome it.

I want to thank Ms. Miasia Jackson, my art teacher, who supported my natural hair and gave me the idea to put my natural hair artwork on t-shirts. I want to thank my supporters of anti-bullying that donated money on my behalf in order to participate in this book:

Victoria Asbury from legalshieldassociate.com/hub/victoriaasbury
Vernell Spann Make-up. New York, NY
Shelagh O'Connor Borgstede from Swank Accessories Boutique. Speonk, NY.

I would like to thank the other contributors of the collaboration. Without you, this couldn't be possible. "If it has to be, let it begin with us."

Finally, I would also like to thank my dad, who has been singing "You are beautiful" to me since I was a little girl, my step-dad, grandmother, and my mom for making my participation in this book possible, and for all the support they gave me; always telling me to keep my head up when I was feeling down, and not to let anyone have the willpower over me to change me, and to answer to only two names - and they are the ones that were given to me at birth. ☺

Justine Adams

****

First, I would like to thank God for helping me this far in my journey and experience of being bullied in my life. Second, I want to thank my mom, grandma and brother (Feona, Dorothy and Timothy) as well as my dear friend Raymond Shine for supporting me in everything that I've done and accomplished. Third, I would like to thank Ms. Katie and the Indian River Public Library staff for welcoming me into their family, as well as supporting me and making me the lead actress in their anti-bullying documentary. Fourth, I want to thank my close loved ones, Mackenzie and Isaiah, for helping me through the good times and bad times and for never giving up on me, and being there for me through thick and thin. I have the best family I could have in my life. Lastly, I want to thank Ms. Sharisa Robertson for allowing me to be a part of this book project with the other young ladies so I could tell my bullying story. Thank you. Thank you. Thank you.

Clara Huff

****

First off, I would like to thank my Father in heaven. I want to thank you for being there and protecting me. I thank God for opening the door for this, and showing me my gift of writing.

Secondly, I'd like to thank my dad, Pastor Carlton Whisonant. You have a great business mind, and if it weren't for your business mind, I probably wouldn't even have thought about this.

Third, my mother, Prophetess Samonia Whisonant, I want to thank you for encouraging me to do this book. I thank you for reminding me that this will help people. Thank you for reminding me that they cannot control me anymore.

Fourth, I would like to thank Miss Sharisa Robertson for allowing me the opportunity to be in this book project! Thank you for letting me becomes a part of this big opportunity to possibly change the world!

I love all of you very much!

Chante N. Whisonant

****

I'd like to thank Ms. Sharisa Robertson for the opportunity to take part in this project. I never really understood how much of a difference I could make until now. I'd like to thank my parents and my granny for encouraging and believing in me. Most importantly, I'd like to actually thank my bullies. Had it not been for what I went through I wouldn't have been able to share my story with others. Hopefully, through my words, I am able to help change someone's mind about bullying others.

Arianna M. Washington

****

I am thankful for God seeing us through everything.

Thank you to my mom for creating this book project and giving us a chance to express ourselves. I hope that others that are being bullied will find their voice, speak up, and not be scared. I hope that those who are bullies get the help that they need.

I thank both my mom and dad for being there for me when I was being bullied. I love you both!!! I want to tell everyone in my family that I love them too.

Good luck to all in the book project and it was great doing this with everyone!

De'Shaia T. Ventour

****

I want to thank you Father God for creating me in His image; I want to thank your son, Jesus Christ, for dying on the cross for my sins, and I want to thank your Holy Spirit for living inside of me and for giving me the power and the words to write this letter.

To my mommy, Darriel S. Anderson, and to my daddy, Larry C. Thurman, thank you for loving me and for being the best parents in the world.

 To all of my family and friends, thank you all for your love, support and prayers.

To my Trinity Community Baptist Church and Kingdom Kids Ministry family, thank you for teaching me about God and how to put Him first in all that I do. For with Him, all things are possible.

Thanks to O.A. Thorp Scholastic Academy and to Circle 4 Success Academic Enrichment Program for empowering me to dream big and to strive for excellence as a King's kid.

A special acknowledgement to Sharisa T. Robertson, a selfless visionary to whom this opportunity would not be possible, thank you for your guidance--God bless you!

Dallas N. Thurman

****

Thanking the highest, God for giving me the gift of life, word and expression. When there was doubt, impossibilities that seemed too much to bear, you took me through my dark days and nights of despair, gave me an open door of direction, protection and love, taking my life to the next level beyond my wildest dreams. You're an awesome God. To my mother, Mary L. Lynch, who is my biggest cheerleader, thank you for your love and prayers. You're the best mom a woman can have. You always let me know that God is always on the throne; I love you. My angel and son, Christopher, who is my biggest motivation and inspiration, I love the young man you are becoming. You have made my life a joy to live, love you. All my relatives and godchildren, (too many to mention), I love you. My village of survival, my ultimate shero, monitor, sister and friend, Mrs. Lucinda Cross, who always makes me cry when I reflect on where and what I was when God sent you in my life, letting me know I am enough and I can make the impossible possible with just one step of faith, and just activate, love ya. Robin Devonish Scott (write it, release it and it will be published lot!), Kim Sudderth, Minister Kim Underwood, The Miller Family, Wendy L. Harvey, Dharma Shakespeare Turner, Caroline Jones, my girl Shalena the Diva Brooster, Arthur KL and Tiffany Belvin, and my new niece Kayelle, Cathy Barnwell, Carol Empress, Poetry Layne, Stephanie Morris, Aminah Cole, LaVerne Newton, Michelle Gill Newton, Brenda L. Graford, all my sisters from the Activate Movement, Tammie and C.J. Williams, Angela Bowman, Stacey Officer Sterling and family, Minister Kathy Elliot, Mrs. Joanne Cambell and family, Mother Gemmel Cunningham, Ambassador Sarita Smiley, my Pastor and First Lady Paul B. Mitchell of Changing Lives Christian Center in Brooklyn, NY, Lithera Forbes, Janell Glenn, David Kayles, my editor and typist, Ms. Phyllis, my besties Selina Spruill Lewis, Eric Young and Bernadette Boyd, my Bayside High School family, AJ Family, and IS59 family (where it all began), One Love. Finally, my sister/friend, Ms. Sharisa Robertson, and all the other fabulous authors on this project - thank you for a God sent opportunity to share my story, wisdom and love to many who are forced into silence. May God bless you! You ROCK! My caretaker, Sandra Shakao - love ya! Whoever I missed, charge it to my head and not my heart.

Author Bonetta Lynch

****

Above all, I want to thank God for bringing me through what he has, and for opening the doors to allow me to take my children out of a situation where my son was being bullied.

Second, I want to thank my mom, Lesia Small, who is not only the greatest mom I have ever met, and the kind of mother I aspire to be, but also my best friend. I would be lost without you!

I want to thank my husband and my children for being the most important people in my life. I love you more than you will ever know!

I also want to thank Sharisa Robertson, for writing such an amazing book to help girls around the world voice their feelings when they feel like they don't have a voice. You are truly an inspiration, and I am so thankful that you allowed me to be a part of this project!

Last, but certainly not least, I want to thank the girls who were brave enough to share their stories in this book. You are all amazing and talented young ladies who have a bright future ahead of you. I'm so impressed by your strength! Never, ever, forget that you're perfect the way you are. Don't let anyone ever convince you otherwise!

Sara Dean

****

Bonus Section for Readers: Add Your Letter

Use the bonus section to add your letter to this book as an unofficial author, and share your letter to your bully, and begin your chapter of having a release and having a voice. There isn't a right or wrong way. Write however you feel. It is OK to be angry, to be scared, even ashamed, but it is even better to get those feelings out of you, especially if you have been holding them in for a long time. Pretend you are in the room with your bully/bullies and you have a chance to say anything, and finally everything, you have wanted to say without any interruptions. What would you say? Write it!

Note: This is just for you, and you can/should also share it with your parents/guardians to have a dialogue about what you wrote and your feelings, but you don't have to show your letter to your bully/bullies. Don't forget to name your letter and come up with a unique closing signature too.

Here are a few base questions to get you started, add to or take away as you feel and need to:

- Why are you being bullied?
- Tell your bully how their behavior affected you, made you feel.
- What do you want from the bully, if anything at all?
- What memories stick out the most from being bullied? What has been done and said to you?
- What do you want to get off of your chest and say to, or ask, your bully?
- How can you stick up for yourself or better handle the situation? How can your parents/teachers/school help?
- How will you move forth from this starting today? How will you turn this into a positive for yourself?
- What do you affirm?

Use the blank page to name your chapter!!!

A Letter To My Bully:

Sticks, Stones, and Words Do Hurt
Theme Song:
"U CAN'T BULLY ME" by TAJ
Download on iTunes or Soundcloud!!!!!!

Made in the USA
Columbia, SC
09 August 2017